PROACTIVE
VOCATIONAL
HABILITATION

Unless Pnc-ll

PROACTIVE VOCATIONAL HABILITATION

by
Eric H. Rudrud, Ph.D.
Department of Psychology
St. Cloud State University

Jon P. Ziarnik, Ph.D.
Gail S. Bernstein, Ph.D.
Rocky Mountain Child Development Center
University of Colorado Health Sciences Center
and
Department of Preventive Medicine and Biometrics
University of Colorado School of Medicine
and
Joseph M. Ferrara, Ph.D.
Department of Special Education
University of South Dakota

·P A U L·H·
BROOKES
PUBLISHING CO.

Baltimore ● London

Paul H. Brookes Publishing Co.
Post Office Box 10624
Baltimore, MD 21204

Typeset by Brushwood Graphics, Baltimore, Maryland.
Manufactured in the United States of America by
The Maple Press Co., York, Pennsylvania.

*HD
7255
.P75
1984*

 # 10277623

03V1335

Library of Congress Cataloging in Publication Data
Main entry under title:

Proactive vocational habilitation.

Includes bibliographies and index.
1. Vocational rehabilitation. 2. Vocational rehabilitation—United
States. I. Rudrud, Eric H., 1950–
HD7255.P75 1984   362'.0425   83-26302
ISBN 0-933716-38-9

Contents

Introduction

Consider the following statistics:

1. Individuals who have been in sheltered workshops for at least 2 years have a 3% chance of being placed in competitive employment (Moss, 1979).
2. Movement within the continuum seems to average 3% annually (United States Department of Labor, 1979).
3. Current national placement and movement data lead to estimates that a mentally retarded adult entering a day activity program will exit to competitive employment in between 47 and 58 years (Bellamy, Rhodes, Bourbeau, & Mank, 1982).

These figures reflect an assumption underlying our present vocational habilitation service delivery system, namely, that competitive employment is impossible for most individuals receiving services.

The vocational habilitation system suggested in this book is based on a very different assumption. We are convinced that competitive employment is a realistic goal for most persons currently receiving vocational habilitation and day training services, and that nearly all other service recipients can expect at a minimum to obtain well-paid supported work. The recent progress that has been made in developing a technology for vocational training of mentally retarded adults has been so impressive that there is now little question of this group's ability to acquire productive vocational skills (Bellamy et al., in press; Bernstein, Ziarnik, Rudrud, & Czajkowski, 1981).

Thus, agencies providing vocational services for handicapped persons must assume the responsibility for consumer success or failure. It is incumbent upon service providers to acquire the skills necessary to assure consumer success. Since mentally retarded individuals constitute the majority of those served in sheltered workshops (United States Department of Labor, 1979), mastery of advances in serving them is central to the provision of effective services.

The contents of this book are based both on the work of recent pioneers in vocational habilitation and on the authors' experiences in consulting with various community-based habilitation programs. In particular, we have been extensively involved with testing the procedures described in the book and are therefore indebted to the Huron Adjustment Training Center in Huron, South Dakota; Goodwill Industries of Denver, Colorado; and the Sioux Vocational School in Sioux Falls, South Dakota.

Many service providers believe that new methods of improving service delivery cannot be implemented without extensive federal support, increased staff, and university graduate students. Our work with the agencies mentioned above suggests otherwise. The only outside supports provided to any of these agencies are occasional small state grants and consultant time and expertise. We are therefore convinced that what is described in this book is both possible and practical.

The intended audience for this text consists of persons responsible for designing and/or providing vocational habilitation services to adults with handicapping conditions. Many of the examples in the book are a reflection of our experiences with mentally retarded or other developmentally disabled persons. However, the approach described for designing effective habilitation services is not specific to any particular handicapping condition and should, therefore, be useful to all professionals in vocational habilitation.

Unit I, Foundations of Proactive Vocational Habilitation, provides the philosophical base for what follows. Chapter 1 reviews proactive principles and discusses the importance of implementing these principles in a vocational program. Chapter 2 describes the characteristics of community-referenced programming as well as its implications for vocational assessment and training strategies. Strategies for developing community-referenced curricula are covered in Chapter 3.

Unit II, Service Delivery Issues, reviews employment-directed service delivery models. Service delivery models in general are covered in Chapter 4. Chapter 5 reviews competitive employment projects that have been reported in the literature, while Chapter 6 is devoted to reducing the gap that exists between the school classroom and vocational training. Throughout, survival in a community job is assumed to be the terminal goal of vocational training.

Unit III, Vocational Evaluation, is devoted to vocational assessment. Chapter 7 reviews the more common vocational evaluation tools and techniques and their advantages and disadvantages. In Chapter 8, a rationale is built for the need for a community-referenced vocational assessment program, and one such program is described.

Unit IV, Survival Skills, addresses problems of curriculum development. Chapter 9 covers vocational survival skills, both generic and specialized, while social survival skills are addressed in Chapter 10.

This book is not a cookbook and does not describe a successful vocational habilitation program because there are many possible successful vocational habilitation programs. Instead, it identifies the questions to be asked and the process to be used in designing a successful program.

Recent research has demonstrated that vocational success is possible for many of the people we serve. *Proactive Vocational Habilitation* is intended to give service providers a model for translating that research into daily service delivery so that the possibility can become a reality.

REFERENCES

Bellamy, G. T., Rhodes, L. E., Bourbeau, P. E., & Mank, D. M. Mental retardation services in sheltered workshops and day activity programs: Consumer outcomes and policy alternatives. Paper presented at the National Working Conference on Vocational Services and Employment Opportunities, Madison, Wisconsin, 1982.

Bernstein, G. S., Ziarnik, J. P., Rudrud, E. H., & Czajkowski, L. A. *Behavioral habilitation through proactive programming*. Baltimore: Paul H. Brookes Publishing Co., 1981.

Moss, J. W. *Post secondary vocational education for mentally retarded adults* (Grant No. 56P 50281/0). Final report to the Division of Developmental Disabilities, Rehabilitation Services Administration, Department of Health, Education and Welfare, 1979.

United States Department of Labor. *Study of handicapped clients in sheltered workshops*, Vol. 2. Washington, DC: United States Department of Labor, 1979.

Acknowledgments

The primary strength of this book, in our view, is that the philosophy, standards, and procedures it describes have all been implemented in existing community-based agencies devoted to service delivery. Several individuals in each setting deserve special thanks.

Dr. Rudrud has been working with the Huron Area Adjustment Training Center in Huron, South Dakota, since 1978. The Huron Vocational Assessment Program would not have been possible without the contributions of Bob Markve and Patty Wendelgass. Appreciation is also due Tom Meekins, Executive Director of Huron Area Adjustment Training Center, and the Section of Special Education, South Dakota Department of Education, for their support of this project.

Drs. Ziarnik and Bernstein have been working with Goodwill Industries of Denver since 1981. Tim Welker, the President, has been consistently supportive of their efforts. Most important, the habilitation program at Goodwill has been implemented by six skilled professionals: Karla Conway, Nina Cruchon, Bob Grupé, Jay Leeming, Cathy Morrison, and Craig Strauss.

Drs. Ferrara and Bernstein have been consulting with the Sioux Vocational School since 1979. Eileen Van Soest and Jim Wick have made the Sioux Vocational School's social-interpersonal skills program a reality.

We also wish to thank the High School Special Education Task Force of Lennox, South Dakota, for many of the ideas presented in Chapter 6. Mary Peterson and her staff have demonstrated how a group of dedicated people can change attitudes and functions within a school.

We are also indebted to Jolene Constance, who typed the final version of the manuscript. She produced consistently excellent results from very rough copy and we were happy to have her working with us.

Finally, we want to say the content of this book has come from working together, sharing ideas, and using each of our experiences and points of view. We are therefore pleased to acknowledge that all the authors contributed equally to this book.

PROACTIVE
VOCATIONAL
HABILITATION

UNIT I

FOUNDATIONS OF PROACTIVE VOCATIONAL HABILITATION

CHAPTER 1

Proactive Principles

OBJECTIVES

To be able to:
1. Define the proactive approach.
2. Identify the advantages of proactive programming.
3. Identify characteristics of proactive client programs.
4. Identify characteristics of proactive staff behavior and knowledge.
5. Identify characteristics of proactive program organization and administration.

At first glance, the proactive approach to habilitation seems deceptively simple. To organize services in a proactive fashion means to anticipate and prevent problems by identifying problem antecedents and consequences and then implementing planned positive solutions (Bernstein, Ziarnik, Rudrud, & Czajkowski, 1981; Ziarnik, 1980). We now know that the proactive approach is both much more difficult to implement and much more useful than we initially imagined when we developed it in the mid seventies as a way of viewing habilitation services. *Proactive* services focus on strengthening desired behavior. Thus, they stand in direct contrast to *reactive* services, which focus on minimizing or reducing a problem after it has occurred. In other words, we want to teach staff to "catch people doing it right" (Houts & Scott, 1975).

Most aspects of the present day human services system are designed to respond to events after they have begun or occurred. A reactive approach is not entirely negative; it does meet many of the "felt needs" of people. Simply stated, felt needs are those problems that people rarely think about until they occur. However, when they do happen, people want immediate solutions. While it is important to solve problems, reactive solutions have certain built-in disadvantages. An entirely reactive approach is relatively costly, inefficient, and self-perpetuating because it generally does not directly or permanently solve problems. For example, using a bucket to catch drips from a leaky roof solves the immediate problem of a wet floor but it does not fix the basic problem of the leak. Isolating a person who is aggressive when upset makes the immediate environment safe for others, but does not teach the person how to behave correctly the next time he or she is upset. Reactivity is solving problems as they come up. This book is devoted to teaching you to identify and proactively solve habilitation problems.

This first chapter introduces you to the implications of the proactive approach as it relates to behavior change programs, staff skills and knowledge, and agency organization.

THE CASE FOR PROACTIVE PROGRAMS

Initially, the concept of proactivity developed because we were concerned about the growing emphasis in both the professional literature and direct service settings on techniques to reduce behaviors. The behavior change literature, particularly as it related to the care and treatment of individuals with handicaps, was often little more than a series of studies that reported on how to reduce a particular response. In these studies, control was exhibited over an undesirable behavior, often without regard to long-term client needs or to the appropriateness of the change technique to applied settings. Thus, with an emphasis in the literature on behavior reduction techniques, it was not surprising that Winett and Winkler (1972) suggested that the goals of most programs seemed to be to develop clients who would "be still, be quiet, be docile" (p. 499). This approach is still practiced all too frequently today. In a statewide survey of programs serving persons with developmental disabilities, we found that carefully documented behavior change programs were used almost exclusively to eliminate undesirable behaviors (Bernstein & Ziarnik, 1982). Why is this a problem, you might ask? Don't undesirable behaviors of clients need to be eliminated? Yes, of course we need to change the problem behaviors, but we believe in accomplishing this via proactive programs that also teach new alternative behaviors. There are several reasons for taking this approach.

First, clients won't necessarily develop positive behaviors on their own. Even though a certain maladaptive behavior has been eliminated, there is no reason to believe that a positive behavior will magically spring forth to take its place. How many times have you eliminated one behavior in an individual only to find another more maladaptive behavior has taken its place? Clients, just like the rest of us, behave as a function of consequences. That is, people engage in inappropriate behaviors that are being reinforced or that result in avoidance of something negative. If you simply eliminate the present undesirable behavior that helps the individual get something good or avoid something bad, he or she will develop new responses in order to maintain the consequences. Rarely are these new responses desirable. Thus, clients must be directly taught positive adaptive behaviors.

Exercise

1-1. When we first met Charlie, he had just entered a community-based vocational program after living for nearly 20 years in the state institution. He was nonverbal but friendly, and staff were impressed by his athletic abilities. Their only real complaint at that time was that Charlie picked up and played with everything that caught his eye. Quite some time later, Charlie came to our attention when the agency requested help in controlling Charlie's behavior. He had begun stealing items of value from a variety of places including community businesses. If not dealt with, Charlie was at risk of being jailed!
   1. What do you think produced this change in Charlie?
   2. What might have been some ways to have avoided it?

Answers to Exercise

1-1. 1. While this is a complex problem with no easy answer, if you guessed that initially Charlie was punished for openly playing with objects without being taught to get what he wanted appropriately, you are on the right track. Charlie learned he had to be sneakier if he was to get what he wanted while avoiding punishment. Over a period of months, Charlie inadvertently learned to steal.
   2. Whatever change techniques you suggested, you *must* include procedures to teach Charlie how to get what he wants in a socially acceptable manner.

A second reason for taking the proactive approach is that focusing on problem behaviors puts the client in charge. When staff wait to apply behavior reduction techniques contingent upon the occurrence of a problem behavior, the client then controls staff responses. Thus, staff are unable to schedule or plan training activities and must wait for "emergencies" to happen before they attempt to change behavior. The most immediate effect of this type of response to problem behavior is that staff feel out of control. Some days, few problem behaviors are exhibited while other days, staff are caught running from one brush fire to the next as they seek to eliminate problem behaviors. Proactive behavior change programs stress planned interventions to teach, increase, or maintain adaptive behaviors (Bernstein et al., 1981). Thus, staff are better able to plan and reduce (if not eliminate) "emergencies." A residential administrator recently wrote to update us on his agency's progress after consultation, saying, "By the way, the next time you state something as crazy as 'I want you to eliminate emergencies,' I for one will not be laughing" (A. Tiger, personal communication, February 17, 1983).

Last, focusing on problem behaviors promotes a negative view of the individual. Compare these reactive goals with proactive goals:

REACTIVE	PROACTIVE
Will not name-call other clients	Will utilize first names when addressing peers
Will not leave work station	Will raise hand and request supervisor assistance
Will reduce time off-task	Will increase time on-task
Will stop complaining	Will name four good things that happened today

If staff constantly view clients as persons who are name-callers, leave their work stations, are off-task, and complain, how can they optimally identify, shape, and reinforce the positive, adaptive behaviors these individuals will need for success in the world? In fact, for staff who view clients in the reactive manner, the job becomes one of maintaining control and daily order rather than providing training, skill development, and habilitation.

CHARACTERISTICS OF PROACTIVE BEHAVIOR CHANGE PROGRAMS

In our vocational program at Goodwill Industries of Denver, we have translated the proactive approach into standards that help guide the development of habilitation programs. Each one of the nine standards listed below will help you in determining how proactive your behavior change programs are.

1. For each client, the majority of habilitation goals are intended to increase adaptive pro-social behaviors. We have consistently recommended that program goals emphasize what the individual needs *to do* instead of what he or she should *not* do (Bernstein et al., 1981; Ziarnik, 1980). That is, goals should be focused on the acquisition of adaptive skills rather than on the elimination of maladaptive behaviors. This is no less true in vocational programs than it is anywhere else, particularly in the area of social skills training. Programming for the elimination of inappropriate social behaviors is not likely to lead to long-term client success. Instead, goals should be designed to teach people what to do instead of the current maladaptive behavior. When evaluating goals for individual trainees, one way to determine whether they are proactive is to apply Ogden Lindsley's "dead man test." This test says, "if a dead man can do it, you probably stated it incorrectly" (O'Brien & Dickinson, 1982, p. 28). For instance, a dead man can reduce time off-task, sit quietly in seat, or reduce noncompliance. The proactive goal is to increase time on-task. In our vocational habilitation program at Goodwill, quarterly evaluation statistics indicate that 95% of all client goals are aimed at increasing or maintaining positive behavior.

2. Client goals relate to a criterion of ultimate functioning. For us, and for numerous other people in the field (e.g., Brown, Nietupski, & Hamre-Nietupski, 1976), the ultimate individual outcome for community-based vocational habilitation is to promote independent client functioning. Therefore, habilitation goals must relate to this criterion. For example, it is hard to see the relationship between matching colors and job success. It is not so difficult to see the relationship between learning to wash floors and success as a janitor, or between increasing interaction skills and independent functioning. By relating habilitation goals to a criterion of ultimate functioning, we force staff to answer the question of *why* we are doing what we are doing.

3. Client goals are directly related to socially valid agency exit criteria. Exit goals are observable descriptions of all the skills trainees must acquire to successfully exit from a training program. Habilitation goals should not be solely related to standardized assessments or to what particular staff *think* an individual needs to learn. Rather, they need to be based on an analysis of what skills and behaviors are necessary for success in the world. Goals must answer the question of where clients are going and what they will have to know and do when they get there (Bernstein et al., 1981). Developing socially valid criteria is emphasized throughout this text.

4. Data that reflect client progress are regularly recorded in each client's file. In our program, staff are required to record data every time a formal behavior change program is implemented. This can happen as frequently as five times a day. Additionally, staff are required to record general case notes utilizing the problem-oriented record format outlined in Bernstein et al. (1981) at least every other week. When initially confronted with documentation requirements, staff frequently believe such requirements will significantly interfere with time spent with clients. This concern is unfounded. In our program, we measure how staff spend their time in job categories such as correspondence, program planning, meetings, on/off work floor client contact, and documentation. Prior to our involvement, staff spent 15% of their time in documentation and 41% of their time in direct client contact. Today, staff spend 35% of their time in data collection and 39% of their time in on work floor client contact. Staff were able to spend 20% more time in documentation by reducing emergencies (accounted for by a decrease in "counseling sessions" that usually occurred off work floor whenever a client displayed undesirable behavior) and by blending data collection with structured training.

5. Data relating to goal attainment are clear and readily understandable. Narrative notations or subjective impressions from various staff are usually less useful than objectively measured data. Subjective judgments are often inaccurate (Kazdin, 1975), while objectively measured data promote consistency in judgment, increase accountability, help determine intervention strategies, and help justify the need for a program (Bernstein et al., 1981). Further, interpretation of subjective narrative data is time-consuming. Visually presented data (e.g., graphic or numerical) enable staff to quickly judge client rates of progress.

6. Baseline data are provided for each habilitation goal. Baseline data are measures of behavior taken *before* a program is implemented. Unless we know where we began, it is impossible to know how far we have come with a given individual. It is not possible to determine progress if pre-intervention behavior is not accurately assessed and recorded. Further, baseline data support the need for a program in the first place. Remember, our subjective impressions are often inaccurate.

7. Program data are available to all staff. All staff who work with clients must know what progress is being made toward goals. As you will see throughout this book, a major focus in proactive programming is the development of socially acceptable behaviors. Because social behaviors by definition occur with a variety of people, it is important that all staff know client priorities, programs, and progress. Shared data facilitate consistent programming by telling staff how to interact with clients.

8. For each goal, a single individual is identified who is responsible for implementing and/or arranging implementation of that goal. One characteristic of the proactive staff person is that he or she "makes decisions and follows through" (Ziarnik, 1980, p. 291). It is hard to track accountability when goals do not identify the person responsible for program implementation, or if they vaguely infer that a group of staff members or the generic supervisor is responsible. If everyone is responsible, then no one is responsible.

9. Where appropriate, habilitation goals are worked on at regularly scheduled times. For each goal, there should be a notation of when the program will be implemented. This needs to be more specific than "Monday in Work Activities." Stating "M-W-F, 9:00–9:15" would be more specific. If we are not specific, we are more likely to forget to implement the program. Where it is not appropriate to schedule a specific program time, it is necessary to document why, as well as what is happening with regard to program implementation.

CHARACTERISTICS OF PROACTIVE STAFF

In addition to developing proactive behavior change programs, we apply the same standards to staff performance. As documented elsewhere, (Bernstein et al., 1981; Ziarnik, 1980), proactive staff view an individual person/problem holistically (i.e., past, present, and future), implement positive solutions, and continually develop their skills while knowing their limits. We have translated these characteristics into behavior and knowledge standards for staff.

Behavior Standards for Staff

1. At least 25% of all interactions with clients involve staff behaviors that are related to client skill acquisition. Behavioral training strategies are the only strategies that have been shown to consistently result in client skill acquisition. Staff must provide modeling, verbal prompts, physical prompts, and positive and negative consequences for clients. There is evidence that very competent staff use these strategies more often than other staff. Utilizing the Behavior Manager Observation System (BMOS) (Bernstein & Ziarnik, 1980), it was found that staff identified by administrators as extremely competent in community-based programs engaged in behavioral training strategies in approximately 28% of all observed interactions with clients. Other staff selected at random from the same programs used these same strategies in only 15% of the observed interactions (Bernstein & Ziarnik, 1982).

   2.   Staff individualize training methods for clients.   What we are interested in ensuring is that staff reinforce different behaviors in different clients using different methods. Not all methods are equally effective for all persons. Some people require physical prompts, while others might resent them. Staff must be sensitive to the needs of the individual.

   3.   Staff provide sufficient amounts of reinforcement.   While there is no absolute standard that allows us to determine how much reinforcement is needed, it is safe to say that reinforcement is sufficient if it produces a positive change in behavior(s). At the skill development level and early in generalization training, we look for a predominantly positive environment. However, to promote maintenance of a behavior, the schedule of reinforcement must be gradually reduced to "natural" levels. Natural levels of reinforcement for many behaviors are either extremely low or indirect. (For example, people rarely directly reinforce social skills by saying, "Good talking." Rather, social contact is maintained.) We have identified the natural levels of reinforcement under which trainees must be able to work by observing real world work supervisors in private industry.

   4.   Staff respond appropriately to both pro-social and maladaptive behaviors in clients.   Behaviors of concern are seldom ignored, though appropriate behaviors are often not positively reinforced. Here, we are looking to see that adaptive behaviors receive consequences that increase the chances of the behavior re-occurring, while maladaptive behaviors receive consequences that decrease their chances of re-occurring. The proportion of behaviors attended to should heavily favor those performed correctly by clients.

Knowledge Standards for Staff

   1.   Staff can state the goals for clients with whom they regularly work.

   2.   Staff can state what progress has been made by clients with whom they regularly work.

   3.   Staff can state individual client histories and how they relate to present and future programs.

   4.   All staff utilize recent articles or other readings relevant to their daily work to improve client programs.   A major problem for direct service staff in community-based programs is the lack of access to literature on habilitation and training, making reinvention of the wheel necessary at regular intervals. Staff must seek information on their own and must be knowledgeable about current state-of-the-art in habilitation training.

Barriers to Staff Proactivity

It is not a particularly startling revelation that people seek to escape or avoid aversive events. What is perhaps new to you is the idea that the termination of an aversive event can be reinforcing. This is called negative reinforcement. In the case of undesirable client behavior, staff have a clearly irritating stimulus that they will attempt to eliminate. There is unfortunately no similar cue for responding to desirable behavior. Too often, staff will try to change a behavior more because it will benefit them (i.e., reduce an aversive stimulus) than because it will benefit the trainee (Loeber, 1975). Remember, the goal of habilitation programs is to teach and increase adaptive behavior, not just to eliminate undesirable behavior. In fact, Loeber (1975) suggested that the definition of an undesirable client behavior should be any behavior that is followed by trainer attempts to reduce or eliminate that behavior.

When staff reactively attempt to reduce aversive stimuli (i.e., undesirable client behavior), they generally choose the quickest, least costly methods. Unfortunately, these are rarely productive or long-lasting. Furthermore, we may actually increase the occurrence of undesirable behaviors by responding reactively.

Exercise

1-2. Every time a staff person walks through the workshop, Jane jumps up from her chair, approaches to within a foot of the individual, and loudly says, "Good morning," while grabbing his or her hand to shake. Most staff respond by answering, whereupon Jane returns to her workplace.
   1. What is maintaining Jane's behavior?
   2. What keeps staff greeting Jane and shaking her hand?

Answers to Exercise

1. If you said that positive reinforcement (in this case, attention) was maintaining Jane's behavior, you are right.
2. If you said negative reinforcement was maintaining the staff's behavior, you are probably right. The staff members have terminated what was for them an aversive stimulus (Jane), by reinforcing an inappropriate response.

Now try to answer these questions:

1. What could you do to proactively change Jane's behavior?
2. How about changing staff?

Answers

1. Jane clearly needs discrimination training in order to learn when, where, and how to greet.

2. Staff also need to know what to reinforce in Jane, and what uniform procedures should be used for dealing with the inappropriate behavior. Additionally, any visitors should be briefed prior to a tour that might bring them in contact with Jane.

As you can see, it is important to remember that the principles of learning relate to staff as well as to clients. If our efforts successfully terminate an aversive stimulus, we will be reinforced. We will likely engage in a similar response when faced with a similar aversive stimulus. Furthermore, when the aversive stimulus is terminated, our response also ceases. A baby cries, the parent picks the child up, the baby quiets, and the parent puts the child down. Marty becomes agitated and upset, his case manager counsels him, Marty becomes calm, and the case manager goes back to other duties. Both the parent and the case manager are controlled by the presence or absence of an aversive stimulus. As you can see, an important issue to consider is: "Who is training whom?"

Example 1.1.

At a Kansas state institution for persons with developmental disabilities, psychologists Bill Eckenroth, Roy Gilliland, and Ray Semrad implemented a token program to increase socially adaptive behaviors and decrease maladaptive behaviors. After several weeks of daily charting the number of tokens distributed for appropriate behaviors and the number of major maladaptive behaviors (such as physical aggression and property destruction), they found the following pattern:

Number of tokens ———
Number of maladaptive behaviors — —

See how increases in the frequency of maladaptive behaviors are followed by increases in the number of tokens distributed daily. Similarly, as maladaptive behaviors decrease in frequency, staff give fewer tokens. One interpretation of these data is that clients have learned that increased rates of maladaptive behavior will result in tokens. This is because staff have been distributing tokens in order to decrease maladaptive behaviors, rather than to increase adaptive behaviors.

In considering barriers to staff proactivity, remember the following points.

1. Too often, trainee behaviors are altered just because they are irritating to staff.
2. Eliminating an undesirable behavior is reinforcing to staff; replacing it with a desirable behavior may not be as reinforcing.
3. Staff behavior can be controlled by client behavior.

CHARACTERISTICS OF THE PROACTIVE AGENCY

In order to provide quality habilitation programs for clients, not only must staff behavior and client programs reflect the proactive approach, but the agency as a whole needs to adopt this model.

Agency Standards

1. The agency has an operationalized goal statement that defines the mission of that agency. A common problem in human services agencies is the attempt to meet too many broad general goals simultaneously. As a result, oftentimes none of the goals are met (Gettings, 1979). The degree to which any agency defines what it offers, for whom, and to what end is directly related to the degree of success in achieving those goals. The agency goal is the conceptual framework from which all actions of the agency follow.

2. The agency has operationalized exit and entrance criteria for each of its programs. Exit and entrance criteria are used to determine who is to be served, how they should be served, and when they have been served. Such criteria answer the question: "Why are these clients here and what do they need to do to get out of here?" (Bernstein et al., 1981). It is easy to keep clients in perpetual training, particularly in programs for developmentally disabled individuals. Exit and entrance criteria not only help agencies to select trainees but also help staff by identifying training content.

3. The agency has a table of organization that accurately reflects actual lines of authority. Management has been defined as achieving production through people (Blake & Mouton, 1964). Therefore, the effective manager delegates both authority and responsibility. A table of organization helps to conceptually organize the authority within a particular agency and identify who is responsible for which function.

4. Each position within the agency has a job description that accurately reflects actual duties and skill requirements for successful performance. Too often, job descriptions involve vague, unoperationalized, or out-of-date statements of duties. In evaluating the adequacy of compliance with this standard, the degree of correspondence between the job description and actual employee responsibilities must be assessed.

5. Performance standards exist for all program staff. In essence, performance standards serve as a method of communicating to staff how they should spend their time and which tasks are priorities. Performance standards that are negotiated with a supervisor represent planned allocation of staff time and effort. Such standards must be observable and measurable and should be developed for all staff. Performance standards are more complex and more difficult to write for high level professional and managerial positions, but they are possible and worth the time and effort required. (For more information on performance standards, see Bernstein et al., 1981.)

6. The agency has a policy statement relating incentives to performance standards. In addition to guiding staff behavior, performance standards can also serve as a feedback mechanism for management because performance can be evaluated against objective criteria. Incentives can be directly related to performance criteria. This implies two responsibilities. First, performance evaluation must be based on operationalized constructive feedback so that staff know how to improve performance. Second, performance standards must be based on desired outcomes, not merely effort. The worthiness of any effort is directly related to the results achieved (Gilbert, 1978).

7. In-house promotion is based on skills that are needed for the new job. Promotion should not be related to technical expertise in the current position or to longevity within the organization (e.g., if you are a good nurse's aide, after a period of time you may be promoted to aide supervisor). Neither of these criteria has any direct relationship to the skills needed for promotion. Lawrence Peter (1975), author of *The Peter Principle,* has suggested that promotion to leadership positions based on the ability to follow (as a subordinate) is as nonsensical as suggesting that the ability to float is related to the ability to sink.

8. The agency has an annual plan for staff development. The plan may utilize in-house resources, outside consultants, or other community resources such as community colleges or universities. In any case, the plan must be based on an annual needs assessment that includes both feedback from staff but also more objective measures such as direct observation of staff performance.

9. The agency holds regular staff meetings with full staff meetings at least monthly and unit meetings more frequently. Staff meetings can serve a valuable function in facilitating communication, increasing staff involvement and commitment, and general information sharing among staff. Full agency staff meetings must have both an agenda specified before the meeting and a mechanism for disseminating meeting content for staff who did not attend. Furthermore, all staff need to be involved in the staff meeting. Too often, in programs providing both day and residential services, staff meetings are held at the convenience of day staff. A mechanism must exist to promote both attendance and involvement of all staff. Most important is the use of staff meetings to jointly solve problems. Little is accomplished if the director is the only speaker at staff meetings.

SUMMARY

Quality habilitation programs are not solely based upon staff qualifications, an effective management system, or the ability to change behavior. In following chapters, we present a system in which quality programs are achieved through the holistic blending of staff and agency structure into a mutually supportive unit with one goal clearly in mind—achieving vocational independence for the persons you serve!

SUGGESTED ACTIVITIES

1. Compare the proactive standards for behavior change programs to programs in your agency. What are the differences? What can be done about them?
2. Try to write at least one behavior change program that meets all the proactive standards.
3. Apply the proactive staff characteristics to yourself. For example, can you name all your clients' goals?
4. Observe other staff working in your agency and compare their behavior to the proactive standards.
5. Present the agency standards in a staff meeting. How does your agency compare? What would it take to change? (You might want to wear armor when doing this.)
6. Write a description of all your present job duties. How does it compare with the "official" description of your job?

REFERENCES

Bernstein, G. S., & Ziarnik, J. P. *The Behavior Manager Observation System (BMOS)*. Paper presented at the annual meeting of the Association for Behavior Analysis, Dearborn, Michigan, May, 1980.

Bernstein, G. S., & Ziarnik, J. P. Proactive identification of staff development needs. *Journal of the Association for the Severely Handicapped*, 1982, 7(3), 97–104.

Bernstein, G. S., Ziarnik, J. P., Rudrud, E. H., & Czajkowski, L. A. *Behavioral habilitation through proactive programming*. Baltimore: Paul H. Brookes Publishing Co., 1981.

Blake, R. R., & Mouton, J. S. *The managerial grid*. Houston: Gulf Publishing Co., 1964.

Brown, L., Nietupski, J., & Hamre-Nietupski, S. *The criteria of ultimate functioning and public school services for severely handicapped students*. Madison: University of Wisconsin and Madison Public Schools, 1976.

Gettings, R. Services to the developmentally disabled: A Washington perspective. In: J. P. Ziarnik (ed.), *Governor's conference on developmental disabilities*. Vermillion: University of South Dakota, 1979.

Gilbert, T. *Human competence: Engineering worthy performance*. New York: McGraw-Hill Book Co., 1978.

Houts, P. S., & Scott, R. A. *How to catch your staff doing something right*. Hershey, PA: Pennsylvania State University, Department of Behavioral Science, College of Medicine, 1975.

Kazdin, A. E. *Behavior modification in applied settings*. Homewood, IL: Dorsey, 1975.

Loeber, R. *The use of behavior modification as an escape from undesirable behavior*. Paper presented at the convention of the American Psychological Association, Chicago, 1975.

O'Brien, R. M., & Dickinson, A. M. Introduction. In: R. M. O'Brien, A. M. Dickinson, & M. P. Rosow (eds.), *Industrial behavior modification*. New York: Pergamon Press, 1982.

Peter, L. *The Peter principle: Why things go always wrong*. Santa Monica, CA: Salinger Educational Media, 1975.

Winett, R. A., & Winkler, R. C. Current behavior modification in the classroom: Be still, be quiet, be docile. *Journal of Applied Behavior Analysis*, 1972, *5*, 499–504.

Ziarnik, J. P. Developing proactive direct care staff. *Mental Retardation*, 1980, *18*(6), 289–292.

Chapter 2

Community-Referenced Programming

OBJECTIVES
To be able to:
1. Define community-referenced vocational programming.
2. Tell why this approach to vocational programming is preferable to other approaches.
3. Identify the implications of the community-referenced approach for vocational assessment and programming.

In order to understand the assumptions behind community-referenced programming, we must first examine the assumptions on which many existing vocational training programs are based. Most of these assumptions are, in fact, myths, and like most myths, they tend to take on a life of their own. That is, they continue to be believed by many people even when there are few logical or scientific reasons for doing so. As we shall see, the assumptions on which a program is based are directly related to client goal selection. If it is assumed that handicapped people cannot be competitively employed, then competitive employment is never selected as a possible goal. Most of the myths described below result in limits on goal selection that are unnecessary and very restrictive for handicapped individuals.

17

THE MYTH OF "READINESS"
(THE MYTH OF THE DEVELOPMENTAL MODEL)

Many training programs assume that normal development is the same as necessary development, which is not the case (Baer, 1973; Wilcox, 1982). This assumption leads to the notion that a disabled individual must acquire skills in the same order as a normally developing individual. For example, one assumption is that the disabled individual will not be "ready" to learn a skill normally acquired at age 16 until the skills normally learned at age 14 have been mastered. The readiness myth often masquerades as the myth of the mental age–chronological age (MA–CA) discrepancy.

The myth of "readiness" does not generally reflect reality even though it may eventually turn out to be true for a few skill sequences under a few conditions. Recent research on vocational training for severely handicapped individuals clearly indicates that individuals with substantial developmental delays can learn age-appropriate vocational skills e.g., Bellamy, Horner, & Inman, 1979; Rusch & Mithaug, 1980; Wehman, 1981). The "readiness"/developmental model/MA–CA discrepancy myth is not supported by the available data.

This myth was scathingly described by Brown, Branston, Hamre-Nietupski, Pumpian, Certo, and Gruenewald (1979):

> For years parents have been told by professionals, "Yes, Mr. Jones, your child is 20 years old and will complete school in 10 months, but he has a MENTAL AGE OF FOUR. That is why we are teaching him to sing, 'When You're Happy and You Know It Clap Your Hands'; that is why we are teaching him to touch long as opposed to short, to touch big as opposed to little, and to touch a card with four pennies taped to it" (p. 81).

THE MYTH OF THE LOCUS OF THE PROBLEM

We are often told that an individual is not making progress because "he's not motivated" or "she could and doesn't want to." Nonsense! It is extremely inappropriate and, more importantly, counterproductive to "blame the victim." Considerable evidence supports the idea that changes in the environment can result in changes in behavior. Thus, the service provider's obligation is to be responsible for changing the situation when an individual is not progressing. In other words, if an individual's program is not successful, change the program instead of blaming the individual (Ziarnik, 1981).

THE MYTH OF PRODUCTION AS THE CRITICAL GOAL

The major focus of many vocational training programs is on improving trainee production. Production that meets competitive standards is certainly an important factor in vocational success. In fact, we will cite research later in this chapter that attests to its importance. However, competitive rates of production by themselves will not result in employment for individuals whose behavior during production is not consistent with social norms. The man who wears stained trousers belted 6 inches above his waist and the woman who shows her anger by pouting every time her supervisor corrects an error are unlikely to be welcomed by employers or fellow employees. Since individuals with handicapping conditions are often singled out for how they look and act, the training of adaptive social skills must be a high priority in any program that successfully teaches people to function in the world at large.

THE MYTH OF QUALITY LIFE

The activities provided by many rehabilitation programs are intended to enrich the quality of life of those served. There is nothing inherently wrong with life enrichment activities. However, these types of activities do not belong in vocational habilitation programs. There are two reasons for excluding such activities from your agency. First, quality of life activities conflict with the primary purpose of vocational habilitation, which is to teach people to be good workers. Employers do not provide field trips, movies, or arts and crafts during the workday, and neither should vocational training programs.

Second, life-enrichment activities are often aimed at teaching skills that are not necessary in vocational settings and must therefore be excluded from our vocational curricula. Given the considerable needs of disabled individuals and the limited resources available to meet them, we must focus on training skills that are directly related to becoming vocationally independent. Other skills that may be desirable but are not necessary can be addressed later in other circumstances. The rationale for doing so has been eloquently developed by Dineen and Sowers (1981):

> By identifying which skills are necessary and which are not, training becomes much more efficient. Many workshops spend a great deal of time during the day attempting to teach time-telling, money counting, reading, and similar skills, instead of focusing on those necessary for work. Retarded persons should have the opportunity to acquire these skills, but the role of the vocational program should be job preparation. In other words, if job placement is not dependent upon the surveyed skills, they should not be taught during the time devoted to vocational training (p. 232).

THE MYTH OF FUNCTIONAL SKILLS

Many training programs base their curricula on the development of functional skills. Unfortunately, the determination of what functional skills are necessary and should be taught is often based on the judgment of the staff in that particular program. One flaw in this approach is that it does not look at the available scientific evidence regarding what skills are in fact needed to succeed in employment as opposed to those skills that are not necessary but might be nice to learn. The second flaw in this approach is that "there is no realistic way to generate an exhaustive list of all the functional behaviors that would serve in any situation" (Bernstein, Ziarnik, Rudrud, & Czajkowski, 1981, p. 43). A third flaw is that a functional skills approach often leads to requirements that all clients be taught cooking, time-telling, and so on, whether they need them or not.

The alternative to the functional skills approach is the critical function approach. This approach requires us to ask for every skill that we teach: a) What is the purpose of this skill?, b) Is it necessary to acquire this skill in order to function in the community?, c) Could the individual function as an adult without it?, and d) Is this skill similar to those encountered in adult life? (Brown, Nietupski, & Hamre-Nietupski, 1976). Probably one of the clearest ways of applying the notion of critical function to vocational habilitation is in regard to the concept of survival. The connection between survival and vocational habilitation is defined by Schutz and Rusch (1982), who describe survival skills as those essential to the acquisition and maintenance of employment. Two types of survival skills are related to successful employment: vocational survival skills and social survival skills. Vocational survival skills are directly related to job performance. Social survival skills directly influence the behavior of others and, while not directly related to productivity, appear to have critical importance for vocational survival (Schutz & Rusch, 1982).

There are many interesting implications of viewing vocational habilitation as the training of survival skills necessary to achieve the critical function of maintaining employment. One is that many goals can be reached in a variety of ways (Bernstein, 1981). For example, there are numerous jobs available in a given community. Any single individual need only acquire the skills necessary for success in one of those jobs in order to become successfully employed.

Another implication of applying the notion of critical function to vocational habilitation is the distinction between making someone employable and making that individual placeable (DuRand & Neufeldt, 1975). Functional skills approaches are directed at training the individual to the point of being employable. On the other hand, the critical function approach has as its goal teaching the individual what is needed in order to become placeable. A community-referenced program is based on the critical function approach. It is aimed at placing the people it serves in employment in the community, not at making those people eligible for employment.

As you can see, whether a vocational program is based on the assumption of critical function or the assumption of functional skills makes a considerable difference with respect to the types of services provided and the goals of the program.

Exercises

Which myth is the basis for each of the arguments listed below?

2-1. Jane isn't working at competitive rates because she isn't money motivated.

2-2. We bus all our clients to the local bowling alley every Friday to help them become more well rounded.

2-3. Tim has to improve his fine motor skills before he can move into the work adjustment program.

2-4. If we can get Sally's production up, maybe she won't babble so much.

2-5. Joe never ties his shoes and is always tripping on the laces. We must teach him shoe-tying.

Answers to Exercises

2-1. Locus of the problem
2-2. Quality of life
2-3. Readiness
2-4. Production as the critical goal
2-5. Functional skills

DEFINING COMMUNITY-REFERENCED VOCATIONAL PROGRAMMING

Community-referenced vocational habilitation programs are based on very different assumptions than the myths described above. These are:

1. The critical function to be achieved is the acquisition and maintenance of employment.

2. The only skills taught are those that are needed to achieve the critical function.

3. All the skills needed to achieve the critical function are taught. For example, social skills or grooming skills may often be taught.

4. The program must fit the client rather than requiring the client to "get ready" for the program.

5. If a client fails, it is because the agency did not provide a satisfactory program. It is therefore the agency's responsibility to provide alternatives.

The sole purpose of a community-referenced vocational training program is to help the people it serves become successfully employed in the local community. By employment, we mean "activity that generates wages and related job benefits, not activity that merely occupies time" (Bellamy, Rhodes, Bourbeau, & Mank, 1982, p. 27). Thus, the success of a vocational habilitation program is measured by: a) the speed and effectiveness with which trainees obtain and maintain competitive employment, or b) employee earnings, benefits, and satisfaction for supported employment programs (Bellamy et al., in press).

This approach assumes that everyone served is capable of working, either in competitive employment or in some sort of supported work situation. Those individuals for whom work is not a goal should not be receiving vocational habilitation services. We assume that a very small group will not have work as a goal. That group will primarily include persons of retirement age.

Some service providers may question whether employment should be a goal for most individuals with handicaps. It seems to us that people with handicaps have a right to become as independent and integrated into their communities as possible. As long as our society equates the independent good citizen with the working taxpayer, to be independent means (unless you are independently wealthy) to be employed. Hence, our advocacy of vocational success as a program goal.

Supported Employment Versus Vocational Habilitation

Most of the vocational habilitation programs we have observed, and/or consulted to, engage in both production and training. That is, they attempt to be both profit-making businesses and training programs. This puts them in the difficult position of trying to make money, pay reasonable wages, hire nearly everyone who is qualified by handicap to work there, and place their best workers with competing firms (Bellamy et al., in press). We are opposed to this sort of arrangement because of the inherent conflicts it produces. In our experience, these conflicts often occur when the need to complete a subcontract by a set deadline can only be met by interfering with habilitation programming. For instance, an individual who has excellent production skills but needs social skills training in relating to co-workers may be required to produce instead of participating in social skills training. On the other hand, consider what happens when an agency that claims to provide both habilitation services and employment runs out of work. Usually, clients must be kept at the agency all day in order for the agency to receive habilitation funding. When this occurs, it is common to see clients either playing games or just sitting.

The solution to these conflicts is to separate vocational habilitation and supported employment. Vocational habilitation programs provide training all day long, regardless of whether paid work is available. Furthermore, in such programs the needs of the clients always take precedence over production.

Supported employment programs are businesses that provide publicly supported jobs for individuals with handicaps but do not provide habilitation services. This definition of supported employment implies that a business that runs out of work will send its employees home; it does not keep them sitting idle with their heads down on a table nor does it give them games to play.

IMPLICATIONS FOR SELECTING PROGRAM GOALS

The definition of community-referenced vocational programming tells us where to look for guidance in selecting program goals. If the purpose of a program is success in employment, the first place to look is the literature on factors related to and/or leading to vocational success. Then, since our focus is on employment in the local community, we must look at jobs in the local community.

Factors Related to Vocational Success

Historically, investigators interested in predicting vocational success, or vocational adjustment, as it is commonly called, have studied formal test measures, the individual's background, and ratings of observable behavior (Krauss & MacEachron, 1982). Studies on characteristics of the individual (e.g., intelligence or sex), and individual history (e.g., length of institutionalization) are unlikely to be of much use to program developers because those variables cannot be changed by program staff. Our interest, therefore, is in scientific studies that have examined the relationship between behaviors that can be changed and vocational success. Specifically, we are interested in four kinds of variables. These are:

1. Work behaviors
2. Vocationally related social skills
3. Other vocationally related skills
4. Characteristics of employment environments

Our primary sources of information on these four types of variables are five recent projects from five different locations around the country. In Nebraska, Schalock and Harper (1978) studied 45 successfully employed handicapped individuals, as well as seven who had been employed but had not succeeded at their jobs. The purpose of the study was to determine what variables discriminated between individuals who were successful and those who were not. Moss (1979) reported on a project in Washington state that trained 63 individuals for competitive employment. His report identifies major reasons for failure when employment was not maintained, as well as those skills included in the curriculum because they appeared to be crucial to vocational success. In Virginia, Wehman and his associates (Hill & Bruff, 1982; Wehman, Hill, Goodall, Cleveland, Barrett, Brooke, Pentecost, & Bruff, 1982) have been training severely handicapped individuals for employment for over 3 years. Recent reports on their program, Project Employability, describe critical variables related to vocational success for 63 clients placed in a total of 75 jobs over a 3-year period. At the end of that period, 42 of the 63 clients (67%) were still working. Krauss and MacEachron (1982) reported the results of training for competitive employment in Massachusetts with 26 mentally retarded adults and examined which variables predicted vocational success. Fifty percent of their sample was successful. Finally, from Ohio, Brickey, Browning, and Campbell (1982) reported on the variables related to failure in competitive employment placements for: a) 64 placements for 53 individuals during 1978, and b) 26 placements made during 1979 and the first half of 1980. Sixty percent of the first group failed, while the failure rate of the second group was unreported.

Work Behavior   Schalock and Harper (1978) noted a significant relationship between working too slowly and failure in competitive employment. The major work-related reasons for failure in Moss's (1979) sample were poor speed and inability to follow instructions. In Project Employability, high quality work and ability to keep working at a constant rate without prompts were related to success on the job (Hill & Bruff, 1982). Brickey et al., (1982) identified low speed and poor quality of work as major work-related reasons for employment failure. Krauss & MacEachron (1982) found successful placement significantly related to task performance, percentage of regular productivity achieved, and the ease of supervision.

Vocationally Related Social Skills   Those social behaviors that appear to be related to failure in employment are:

1.   Inappropriate behaviors (Schalock & Harper, 1978)
2.   Poor social relationships and inappropriate verbal behaviors (Moss, 1979)
3.   Noncompliance with supervisors (Wehman et al., 1982)
4.   Poor peer relationships, inappropriate behaviors, poor relations with supervisors, and poor motivation (Brickey et al., 1982).

Note that all the relationships between social skills and employment were described by the investigators in terms of what the people who failed did incorrectly. Before research results can be useful for proactive program planning, we must identify what the successful employees did correctly.

Other Vocationally Related Behaviors   While there are other behaviors that appear to be somewhat related to vocational success or failure, the available results in this area must be interpreted very cautiously. This is because the relationships that have been found to exist are much weaker than the relationships of the above-mentioned variables to unsuccessful competitive employment. For instance, Schalock and Harper (1978) found that 14% of their unsuccessful placements had deficits in money management, communication, personal appearance, and/or health. Moss (1979) identified poor hygiene as a minor contributor to failure, as have Brickey et al. (1982). The one other related variable that does appear to make a fairly significant contribution to success or failure in competitive employment is absenteeism and/or tardiness (Brickey et al., 1982; Krauss & MacEachron 1982; Wehman et al., 1982). Absenteeism and tardiness problems are often the result of faulty training in following a schedule, failure to use public transportation effectively, or unpredictability of the person providing rides to work (Wehman et al., 1982).

Characteristics of Employment Environments   Krauss and MacEachron (1982) report the only results in the area of work environments. They found that the amount of the hourly wage paid, the amount of bonus or bonuses received, and the employer's commitment to hiring handicapped individuals were significantly related to successful placement. While it is unlikely that these factors can be varied within a particular job setting, further research along these lines may suggest variables that may aid in the selection and/or screening out of prospective employers.

Now, what does all this mean in terms of selecting program goals? At the moment, what these findings do is to provide direction with respect to areas of emphasis in vocational programs. The available evidence is obviously scanty at this time, and program directors should continuously review the scientific literature for new findings in this area. Nonetheless, the findings reviewed above suggest the following areas of emphasis for vocational habilitation programs: attendance, punctuality, work speed, work quality, response to supervision, and social interactions on the job.

Community Referencing of Program Goals

In a community-referenced vocational training program, training outcomes are matched to the skills required for jobs available in the local community (Rudrud, 1981). Therefore, every vocational habilitation program must be based on a thorough assessment of what jobs are available in the local community. There are at least two ways of doing this. One is to compile figures over time from the local job service agency in order to determine what proportion of jobs available fall into each of a variety of categories (Rudrud, 1981). Another alternative is to analyze several editions of Sunday want ads in a major local paper and determine what proportions of listings fall into each job category. In either case, information about what is available needs to be considered along with seasonal and economic trends.

Identifying Component Skills The process that has just been described is the first step in what is known as the survey-train-place model (Schutz & Rusch, 1982). This model involves identifying possible jobs, training people in the needed skills (either on the job or prior to entry to the job), and placement in the job. An important component of the survey step in the survey-train-place model is the process of identifying the component skills involved in a particular job. In other words, we need to know what someone has to be able to do in order to succeed in a particular kind of employment. Rusch, Schutz, and Agran (1982) have described at least two approaches to obtaining the needed information. The first is called *descriptive validation*. This means you ask someone who knows the job, such as the employer or someone actually performing the job, to describe the skills needed. The second approach is called *comparative validation*. Comparative validation involves comparing the behavior of your trainees with the behavior of people actually employed in this particular job to determine what current workers do that trainees need to learn to do. Also of primary importance is the identification of the conditions under which the necessary skills must be performed. These include types of settings, kinds of supervision conditions, and types of reinforcement conditions, among others (Alper & Choisser, 1981).

Direct Observation Direct observation can also be used to identify skills needed for vocationally related behaviors, such as job interviewing skills. Hill, Wehman, and Pentecost (1980) identified necessary job interview skills by having staff observe actual interviews with previously placed clients. The staff identified what pro-social behaviors were demonstrated during the interview (e.g., shaking hands). The staff also questioned employers on what clients did that made them uncomfortable, as well as observing what client behaviors resulted in the employer turning to speak to the staff person rather than the client.

Environmental Inventory Another approach to the survey process is the environmental inventory described by Wilcox and Bellamy (1982). This involves direct inspection of the actual environment in order to analyze it for performance demands and naturally occurring cues and consequences. Wilcox and Bellamy (1982) suggest that the process of prioritizing program goals should be determined by the frequency and/or importance of the target behaviors in the employment environment.

Exercises

2-6. What are the implications of the available research on factors related to vocational success for vocational habilitation programs?

2-7. What are the steps involved in community referencing the objectives of a vocational training program?

Answers to Exercises

2-6. The implications are that trainees must be taught to produce high quality work at high rates, attend regularly and punctually, take supervision, and engage in adaptive social behaviors on the job.

2-7. Identify what jobs are available in your community. Then identify the skills needed to succeed in those jobs, the conditions under which the jobs must be performed, and the quality standards that must be met.

COMMUNITY-REFERENCED ASSESSMENT AND TRAINING

Community-Referenced Assessment

Standardized vocational evaluation instruments, such as the Valpar Component Work Sample Series, the TOWER System, or the Wide Range Employment Sample Test, are unlikely to be useful in a community-referenced training program. There are a number of problems with these types of instruments that are discussed in Chapter 7. Basically, standardized instruments may not reflect the types of jobs that are available and the skills that are necessary for those jobs in your community. Therefore, in order to determine what skills trainees have and what they need to acquire, any appropriate assessment instrument must be

based on the community's criteria for judging someone's fitness for employment. An extensive example of how this can be accomplished is presented in
Chapter 8.

Community-Referenced Training

The training strategies employed by a community-referenced vocational habilitation program have three characteristics: a) they are effective, b) they promote
generalization, and c) they are socially valid.

Effective Training Strategies There tends to be entirely too much
emphasis on the administrative structure of many vocational training programs
at the expense of emphasis on the actual training strategies used by staff. The
most elegant curriculum provided in the most impressive building will not
necessarily result in successful training unless cues and consequences are
effectively delivered. Staff members must be familiar with and skilled in
actually using, on a regular basis, the best currently available training strategies
in order for training to be as effective as possible. There are several excellent
descriptions of well-researched effective training strategies that should form
the basis for the library at any good vocational training program for handicapped persons: Bellamy, Horner, and Inman (1979); Bernstein et al. (1981);
Mithaug (1981); Rusch and Mithaug (1980); Wehman (1981) and Wehman and
McLaughlin (1980).

Generalization A major barrier to the success of severely disabled
individuals is their failure to generalize or transfer acquired skills from one
situation to another. Unfortunately, many vocational programs are based on
faulty assumptions about the ability of trainees to generalize. For instance, it is
often assumed that behaviors exhibited during vocational evaluation are similar
to the behaviors that will be exhibited during vocational placement, or that
attention to task will be the same across a variety of very different tasks. These
assumptions cannot be taken for granted, particularly with more severely
impaired individuals. In fact, probably the best assumption is: Don't assume
anything. The implication of not assuming anything is that we must deliberately
program for generalization of skills rather than taking the more traditional
"train and hope" approach (Stokes & Baer, 1977).

Several rules of thumb have been formulated that will help guide generalization programming. They are:

1. Whenever possible, train in the natural setting. Artificial instructional
settings do not allow severely handicapped individuals to solve real life
problems or perform practical skills (Brown et al., 1976). This means that
programs occurring exclusively in classrooms and simulated activities are
clearly inadequate for developing adaptive skills (Wehman & Hill, 1982).
Many cues and settings in the community cannot be provided in sheltered
training situations. Therefore, a population that has trouble generalizing
needs training in the real context (Wehman & Hill, 1982).

2. Whenever possible, train using natural materials and tasks. One of the biggest mistakes made in most sheltered workshops is an in-house reliance on contract work, most of which involves sitting and doing some kind of assembly work. Most job placements, however, are made in areas such as janitorial and food service. It is not reasonable to assume that severely disabled individuals will generalize high productivity from sheltered workshop contracts to food service settings (Wilcox, 1982).

3. Use real materials. As with commercially available vocational evaluation, standardized curriculum materials are unlikely to be useful in a particular community (Brown et al., 1976). Similarly, arts and crafts are not equivalent to vocational skills training (DuRand & Neufeldt, 1975). Don't have your trainees making pots with clay unless there are jobs available in your community to do just that.

4. Emphasize group instruction rather than one-to-one instruction. While some one-to-one instruction is probably necessary, it is a grave mistake to teach trainees to be dependent on the total attention of a trainer in order to learn (Brown et al., 1976).

5. Program for consistent inconsistency (Brown et al., 1976). One of the biggest complaints training programs have about handicapped individuals is that they are not flexible. Handicapped people are not innately inflexible. We teach them to be inflexible by providing them with very structured routines that remain the same day after day. People whose environments consistently have a certain amount of inconsistency in them learn to be flexible.

Programming for generalization is much more likely to result in success than the usual culmination of the "train and hope" approach (Stokes & Baer, 1977), which is "place and pray" (Usdane, 1976).

Socially Valid Training Strategies   Social validation is the process of determining: a) if goals are socially meaningful, b) if the procedures used to achieve those goals are socially acceptable, and c) if the effects or amount of change achieved are socially important (Wolf, 1978). The selection of community-referenced training goals is in itself a social validation process, since the purpose of community referencing is to select socially meaningful goals.

We are also interested in having socially acceptable training procedures. There are a variety of reasons for this. Probably the most compelling is that, as much as possible, training should occur in the setting where the skills to be acquired must be performed. This means taking vocational habilitation programs out into the community. If we do so, we may find that some effective training strategies are not socially acceptable. For instance, Menchetti, Rusch, and Lamson (1981) assessed the acceptability of various behavior change procedures in competitive employment settings. They also evaluated whether varying descriptions of the trainees would affect the acceptability of these procedures. For example, while 57% of those surveyed would allow the use of a golf counter to take data on a handicapped person's performance, only 29% would allow the same procedure for a nonhandicapped person. The results of this study illustrate the necessity of validating training strategies that will be used in the community.

Furthermore, many vocational training programs conduct numerous tours of their facilities for advocates, parents, legislators, and other interested parties. Therefore, it is also a good idea to socially validate training strategies that will be used within nonintegrated training programs. When the goal of service is the integration of disabled persons into the community at large, social validation of the training strategies used will help promote that integration.

Finally, the amount of change achieved must be socially important in order for training to be successful. For example, suppose a man responds to every constructive criticism from his supervisor by screaming, "Leave me alone!" After he is trained in adaptive ways to handle constructive criticism, he listens carefully and says, "Okay," two out of three times. However, one-third of the time he still screams. This is an improvement, but he probably has not changed enough to meet society's expectations. Thus, the change is not yet socially important.

SUGGESTED ACTIVITIES

1. Identify the assumptions on which your training program is based. Are any of them myths?
2. List the ways in which your program is community referenced and the ways in which it is not. Discuss with your colleagues how to change the ways your program is not community referenced.
3. Observe what training strategies are used by your training staff. Determine whether these strategies: a) are effective, b) promote generalization, and c) are socially valid.

REFERENCES

Alper, S., & Choisser, L. Community-referenced vocational assessment of the severely handicapped. *Vocational Evaluation and Work Adjustment Bulletin,* 1981, *14,* 70–73.

Baer, D. M. The control of the developmental process: Why wait? In: J. R. Nesselroade & H. W. Reese (eds.), *Life-span developmental psychology: Methodological Issues.* New York: Academic Press, 1973.

Bellamy, G. T., Horner, R. H., & Inman, D. P. *Vocational habilitation of severely retarded adults.* Baltimore: University Park Press, 1979.

Bellamy, G. T., Rhodes, L. E., Bourbeau, P. E., & Mank, D. M. *Mental retardation services in sheltered workshops and day activity programs: Consumer outcomes and policy alternatives.* Paper presented at the National Working Conference on Vocational Services and Employment Opportunities, Madison, Wisconsin, 1982.

Bernstein, G. S. On selecting target behaviors: How many ways are there to get where we're going? *Division 25 Recorder,* 1981, *16,* 7.

Bernstein, G. S., Ziarnik, J. P., Rudrud, E. H., & Czajkowski, L. A. *Behavioral habilitation through proactive programming.* Baltimore: Paul H. Brookes Publishing Co., 1981.

Brickey, M., Browning, L., & Campbell, K. Vocational histories of sheltered workshop employees placed in projects with industry and competitive jobs. *Mental Retardation,* 1982, *20,* 52–57.

Brown, L., Branston, M. B., Hamre-Nietupski, S., Pumpian, I., Certo, N., & Gruenewald, L. A strategy for developing chronological age-appropriate and functional curricular content for severely handicapped adolescents and young adults. *Journal of Special Education,* 1979, *13,* 81–90.

Brown, L., Nietupski, J., & Hamre-Nietupski, S. Criterion of ultimate functioning. In: M. A. Thomas (ed.), *Hey, don't forget about me.* Reston, VA: Council for Exceptional Children, 1976.

Dineen, J. P., & Sowers, J. Client rights of the developmentally disabled in vocational settings. In: G. T. Hannah, W. P. Christian, & H. B. Clark (eds.) *Preservation of client rights.* New York: The Free Press, 1981.

DuRand, J., & Neufeldt, A. H. *Comprehensive vocational service systems.* Toronto: National Institute on Mental Retardation, 1975.

Hill, M., & Bruff, B. A three-year analysis of supervisor evaluations of severely disabled workers. In: P. Wehman & M. Hill (eds.), *Vocational training and placement of severely disabled persons* (Vol. 3). Richmond: Virginia Commonwealth University, 1982.

Hill, J. W., Wehman, P., & Pentecost, J. Developing job interview skills in mentally retarded adults. *Education and Training of the Mentally Retarded,* 1980, *15,* 179–186.

Krauss, M. W., & MacEachron, A. E. Competitive employment training for mentally retarded adults: The supported work model. *American Journal on Mental Deficiency,* 1982, *86,* 650–653.

Menchetti, B. M., Rusch, F. R., & Lamson, D. S. Social validation of behavioral training techniques: Assessing the normalizing qualities of competitive employment training procedures. *Journal of the Associaton for the Severely Handicapped,* 1981, *6,* 6–16.

Mithaug, D. E. *Prevocational training for retarded students.* Springfield, IL: Charles C Thomas, 1981.

Moss, J. W. *Post-secondary vocational education for mentally retarded adults.* Reston, VA: Council for Exceptional Children, 1979.

Rudrud, E. H. Job openings and client placements: Over and under met needs. *Vocational Evaluation and Work Adjustment Bulletin,* 1981, *14,* 80–82.

Rusch, F. R., & Mithaug, D. E. *Vocational training for mentally retarded adults.* Champaign, IL: Research Press, 1980.

Rusch, F. R., Schutz, R. P., & Agran, M. Validating entry-level survival skills for service occupations: Implications for curriculum development. *Journal of the Association for the Severely Handicapped,* 1982, *7,* 32–41.

Schalock, R. L., & Harper, R. S. Placement from community-based mental retardation programs: How well do clients do? *American Journal on Mental Deficiency,* 1978, *83,* 240–247.

Schutz, R. P., & Rusch, F. R. Competitive employment: Toward employment integration for mentally retarded persons. In: K. P. Lynch, W. E. Kiernan, & J. A. Stark (eds.), *Prevocational and vocational education for special needs youth: A blueprint for the 1980s*. Baltimore: Paul H. Brookes Publishing Co., 1982.

Stokes, T. F., & Baer, D. M. An implicit technology of generalization. *Journal of Applied Behavior Analysis*, 1977, *10*, 349–367.

Usdane, W. The placement process in the rehabilitation of the severely handicapped. *Rehabilitation Literature*, 1976, *37*, 162–165.

Wehman, P. *Competitive employment: New horizons for severely disabled individuals*. Baltimore: Paul H. Brookes Publishing Co., 1981.

Wehman, P., & Hill, J. W. Preparing severely handicapped youth for less restrictive environments. *Journal of the Association for the Severely Handicapped*, 1982, *7*, 33–39.

Wehman, P., Hill, M., Goodall, P. A., Cleveland, P., Barrett, N., Brooke, V., Pentecost, J., & Bruff, B. Job placement and follow-up of moderately and severely handicapped individuals: An update after three years. In P. Wehman & M. Hill (eds.), *Vocational training and placement of severely disabled persons* (Vol. 3). Richmond: Virginia Commonwealth University, 1982.

Wehman, P., & McLaughlin, P. J. *Vocational curriculum for developmentally disabled persons*. Baltimore: University Park Press, 1980.

Wilcox, B. Forum—Mastering pre-requisite skills: The "readiness" logic. *TASH Newsletter*, 1982, *8*, 1–2.

Wilcox, B., & Bellamy, G. T. *Design of high school programs for severely handicapped students*. Baltimore: Paul H. Brookes Publishing Co., 1982.

Wolf, M. M. Social validity: The case for subjective measurement or how applied behavior analysis is finding its heart. *Journal of Applied Behavior Analysis*, 1978, *11*, 203–214.

Ziarnik, J. Preparing MR adolescents for successful societal adaptation. In: N. Anastasiow (ed.), *New directions for exceptional children: Socioemotional development* (No. 5). San Francisco: Jossey-Bass, 1981.

CHAPTER 3

Community-Referenced Curricula

OBJECTIVES

To be able to:
1. Define community-referenced curriculum.
2. List the differences between a community-referenced curriculum and other curricula.
3. List the steps utilized in developing a community-referenced curriculum.
4. Use the three-column format to describe skills to be taught.
5. Define task analysis, shaping, prompting, fading, and chaining.

The purpose of this chapter is to describe the general process by which a community-referenced curriculum is developed and implemented. Specific examples of various aspects of the process are described in Chapters 8, 9, and 10.

A community-referenced curriculum is intended to help teach people the skills they need to become as independent as possible in their home communities. A community-referenced curriculum must therefore answer the proactive question: Where is this person going? In other words, curriculum content should be directly related to where a person is going and what skills and behaviors are needed to get there and stay there (Bernstein, Ziarnik, Rudrud, & Czajkowski, 1981).

CHARACTERISTICS OF THE
COMMUNITY-REFERENCED CURRICULUM

Community-referenced curricula differ from other curricula in several important ways. The most important difference is that community-referenced curricula are designed to teach skills useful for achieving critical functions, not functional skills. Thus, community-referenced programs often reject traditional curriculum domains such as reading, writing, and arithmetic, and teach skills that are derived from the basic demands of adult functioning such as vocational skills, mobility, and independent living skills (Bellamy & Wilcox, 1982). Your program may be teaching any number of things, but unless what you teach has been shown to be directly related to increased independence, you are not teaching skills that achieve a critical function. Furthermore, a community-referenced curriculum is based on the assumption that a critical function can often be achieved in more than one way (Bernstein, 1981). For example, one criterion we use for entry into community employment in our Denver program is that the individual be able to independently care for personal hygiene. We recently worked with an individual who was catheterized for urination and could not care for herself alone. Solution? This individual used earnings to pay for an aide to come to the workplace daily and assist her. Note that the entry criterion requires that the person be able to care for himself or herself *independently*, not *alone*. An example of a situation where a skill is being taught without regard for critical function was described by Wehman (1983): "It breaks my heart to see a grown man in an activity center who's working to learn to tie his shoes. Buy the man some loafers and drive on!" (p.2).

The second difference is that community-referenced curricula are socially valid while most other curricula are not. That is, we find out directly whether it makes any difference to society if people learn a particular skill. For example, one of the ways the exit criteria from our vocational program at Goodwill Industries were developed was to ask community employers what work skills were of critical importance. Third, a community-referenced curriculum is age-appropriate. In contrast, Brown, Pumpian, Baumgart, Vandeventer, Ford, Nisbet, Schroeder, & Gruenewald (1981) pointed out that most curricula offered to severely handicapped students through age 21 are designed to teach them how to function as nonhandicapped children under the age of 5. Since severely handicapped students manifest significant skills deficits, they too frequently receive instruction only on curriculum objectives characteristically offered to infants or very young children.

Fourth, the community-referenced curriculum does not utilize longitudinal or developmental sequences. What curricula exist are usually based on theories or models of normal human development. The developmental model assumes skills and abilities are mastered in sequential steps and it is necessary to master each skill in sequence before learning the next skill. Remember, as we noted in Chapter 2, normal development is not the same as necessary development (Baer, 1973). Curriculum models that are based on normal development are useful only if students make reasonable progress through hierarchies, sequences, stages, and concepts. Unfortunately, severely disabled students rarely, if ever, progress through such hierarchies at rates justifying the longitudinal use of such models.

Fifth, the community-referenced curriculum trains needed skills directly. For example, if an individual needs training in a vocational task such as sorting, the trainer utilizing a community-referenced curriculum does not focus on figure-ground relationships, sequential patterning, and general eye-hand coordination. Rather, the training is provided on the appropriate dimension being sorted (e.g., shape, color, or size).

Finally, a community-referenced curriculum will continually change as the community changes (Wilcox & Bellamy, 1982). As new vocational opportunities, living arrangements, transportation systems, and leisure activities become available, revisions in the curriculum must occur. Commitment to a community-referenced curriculum requires commitment to an ongoing process rather than to a static and final product.

Exercises

3-1. Define community-referenced curriculum.
3-2. List the six differences between a community-referenced curriculum and other curricula.

Answers to Exercises

3-1. A community-referenced curriculum is a curriculum that helps people achieve independence and answers the questions: "Where are you going?" and "What will you need when you get there?"
3-2. Community-referenced curricula differ from other curricula in that:
   a. community-referenced curricula reject traditional curriculum domains, and employ categories that are derived from the basic demands of adult functioning.
   b. Community-referenced curricula are socially valid.
   c. Community-referenced curricula are age-appropriate.
   d. Community-referenced curricula do not utilize longitudinal or developmental sequences.
   e. Community-referenced curricula train needed skills directly.
   f. Community-referenced curricula continually change as the community changes.

DEVELOPMENT OF COMMUNITY-REFERENCED CURRICULA

What About Packaged Curricula?

The utility of packaged curricula is usually very limited because: a) they include skills not relevant to your community, and/or b) they do not include relevant skills critical to survival in your community. Rudrud, Ferrara, Wendelgass,

Markve, and Decker (1982) investigated the effectiveness of community-referenced procedures as compared to packaged curriculum for informing developmentally disabled individuals about job options within the community. The community-referenced procedures resulted in clients having a better understanding about job requirements. The packaged job-counseling materials provided only general information about occupations and very limited knowledge about job specifics.

Thus, we must be leery when adopting commercially available materials. Wilcox and Bellamy (1982) point out that curriculum materials for both regular and special populations are usually designed for a universal audience. This means that the same objectives taught in the same sequence are assumed to meet the universal needs of all people in all places. This universal approach does not take into account unique individual and community variables.

Packaged curricula are also limiting in a second way. By using exhaustive lists of skills and behaviors, and attempting to teach everything to everyone, we often keep individuals in perpetual training and lose sight of the fact that there is a world that they need to enter. Many handicapped people are excluded from more independent lifestyles because of failure to master noncritical skills. No one needs to master the skills for all possible vocational, leisure, and residential options in his or her community. How many people can perform every job in the community? Instead, what is important is that each individual have sufficient skills to hold one or two jobs, live in one or two residential arrangements, spend his or her free time constructively, and have maximum independence in areas of personal management (Ziarnik, 1981).

Curriculum Development

This section describes the steps involved in developing a community-referenced curriculum. While subsequent chapters discuss specific applications to vocational habilitation, the general approach can be applied to other sorts of programs as well.

1. Identify the critical function. In other words, answer the proactive questions: "Where are these people going?" and "What do these people need to change to get out of here?"

2. List all the possible ways to achieve that function. Remember that critical functions can almost always be achieved in more than one way.

3. Decide how your curriculum will achieve the critical function. There are usually practical reasons to consider when deciding how your curriculum will achieve critical function. For instance, in a large city, bus riding is usually the preferred method of traveling to work because cabs are too expensive and hitchhiking is unreliable. In a rural community, however, bike riding may well be the preferred method. This step can be thought of as delineating the curriculum domain (Brown, Branston, Hamre-Nietupski, Pumpian, Certo, & Gruenewald, 1979).

4. Delineate natural environments. The rationale for delineating natural environments is to identify where the skills to be taught are likely to be needed (Brown et al., 1979). Since specific skills can be performed in any one of many environments, the task here is to list those possible environments and the requirements for each. When doing this, it is not alway easy to decide how many possible environments to choose. For example, it would be of little purpose to teach an individual to operate all the different types of laundromats in his or her community when that person is only likely to utilize the one nearest to his or her residence. However, learning to cross numerous types of streets (e.g., one-way streets, streets with traffic signals, streets without crosswalks) would increase independence, while only learning to cross those on the way to work would be restrictive.

5. Delineate the needed components of each skill to be learned, the conditions under which each component must be performed, and the criterion for completion of each component. Validation of the skills to be learned as described in Chapter 2 is a part of this process.

Exercise

3-3. List the five steps utilized in developing a community-referenced curriculum.

Answer to Exercise

3-3. 1. Identify the critical function.
2. List all the possible ways to achieve that function.
3. Decide how your curriculum will achieve the critical function.
4. Delineate natural environments.
5. Delineate the needed components of each skill to be learned, the conditions under which each component must be performed, and the criterion for completion of each component.

**INSTRUCTIONAL PROCEDURES
USEFUL WITH COMMUNITY-REFERENCED CURRICULA**

The remainder of this chapter is devoted to a variety of general behavioral/ instructional procedures useful for implementing community-referenced curricula, with special emphasis on task analysis. The procedures described here have all been shown to contribute to successful habilitation. However, these procedures alone, no matter how well used, will not result in positive outcomes. The reason they are insufficient is that all involve what to do before the desired behavior occurs. The effective use of consequences must also be an integral part of the training you provide if you wish to ensure trainee success. That is, what happens after a behavior occurs will determine whether or not the behavior continues to occur. The details of effective consequence use can be found in Bernstein et al. (1981), as well as in any good behavior-management text.

Task Analysis

One instructional technique for implementing community-referenced curricula is the use of task analysis. A task analysis breaks a task down into specific component skills, each of which is essential for completion of the task. Component skills are written as instructions to the trainee. Task analysis has been demonstrated to be a critical element of successful training. For instance, in a study of the relationship between successful training of severely handicapped students and 86 variables, use of task analyzed programs was one of the two major contributors to student achievement (Fredericks, Anderson, Baldwin, Grove, Moore, Moore, & Beaird, 1977).

In task analysis, training can be thought of as building a chain of specific responses or behaviors. For example, the task of cleaning up a work area is not one behavior; rather, it is many separate behaviors including returning tools to designated places, checking the floor, cleaning the floor, throwing away trash, and returning any unused materials. Each response in the chain is cued by a different stimulus. The clock or whistle indicating quitting time serves as a cue for returning tools to a designated place. Additionally, each response of the chain also serves as a cue for the next response. For example, checking the floor and finding it dirty is a cue for getting a broom to sweep up the dirt. Each step cues a successive response until a clean work area has been achieved.

When developing a task analysis, the scope of the main task should be limited. For example, it is not feasible to develop a task analysis for working. Instead, working should be broken down into its component parts such as attendance, on-task, response to supervisor, and following safety rules. While any task can be correctly performed in a variety of ways, the task analysis should be designed to make the task as easy to learn as is possible. There are four basic rules that should be utilized:

1. Minimize the number of different discriminations to be made. For example, in a complex assembly task, place component parts in bins that are ordered in the way the parts are assembled rather than having the client sort as well as assemble.
2. Use a unique set of stimuli to cue each response. For example, do not use the cue "put the work on the table" if there are several types of work. Effective cues focus on what is unique about the stimulus.
3. Teach the general case before teaching the exceptions. For example, you cross the street on the green light except when you hear an emergency vehicle approaching.
4. Maximize the use of concepts and operations that the trainee has already learned. For example, if the trainee already knows "big" and "little," do not use "large" and "small" as cues when teaching a task requiring size discrimination.

Development of the Task Analysis After breaking a task down into component skills, the next step is to develop the task analysis. The subtasks must be written in observable terms and focus on what the learner will do. These become the steps of the task analysis. Moyer and Dardig (1978) outlined several ways to develop task analyses. These include:

1. *Watch a master perform.* The basic procedure is to watch a person who is proficient in the performance of the task complete it. As each step is completed, write down in correct order all steps performed.
2. *Perform the task yourself.* Performing the task yourself is a very useful technique but it may become difficult to stop the task and write down all of the steps. Repeating descriptions of each step into a tape recorder can be helpful here.
3. *Work backward through the task.* Often, when constructing a task analysis, staff are too familiar with the task and as a result omit certain key steps when writing the analysis. One procedure that may help to reduce these oversights is to start at the end and work backwards through the task.
4. *Brainstorming.* Group brainstorming is extremely useful for analyzing complex tasks that are not always performed in the same way, such as making change for a dollar or purchasing clothing. Several staff members should get together and write down all identified subtasks and then arrange the subtasks in a logical order.
5. *Break down complex patters of behavior.* Breaking down complex patterns of behavior is used most successfully with behaviors from the affective domain (Moyer & Dardig, 1978). For example, we may view self-confidence as consisting of component behaviors such as self-reinforcement, responding to praise, erect posture, and exploring new situations. These component behaviors collectively result in the attainment of the goal of self-confidence. The purpose is not to arrive at a sequential list of behaviors, but rather to identify the individual behaviors that collectively result in goal attainment.

Task Analysis and Data Recording Figures 3.1 and 3.2 are examples of task analyses on data sheets. This format allows the recording of progress for individuals learning the behavior chains shown, which are task analyzed skills.

Exercise

3-5. Define task analysis and list five procedures that can be used to develop a task analysis.

Answer to Exercise

3-5. A task analysis breaks down a task into its specific components or subskills. A task analysis can be developed by using the following

Task Analysis Data Sheet

Program __Return to work after break__   Scoring summary:
Client _____   3—without assistance
Instructor _____   2—verbal prompt
Reinforcers _____   1—gestural/imitative
Materials _____   0—physical prompt
Task statement " __Return from break__ "

Dates

When you are sitting in the break room and the bell rings									
1. Stand up									
2. Push chair in									
3. Walk downstairs									
4. Walk to work station									
5. Sit down									
6. Begin work									
7.									
8.									
9.									
10.									
11.									
12.									
13.									
14.									
15.									
16.									
17.									
18.									
19.									
Number of steps scored 3:									

Figure 3.1. Task analysis—Return from break.

Task Analysis Data Sheet

Program ___Increase problem-solving ability___

Client _____

Instructor ___Nina Cruchon_____

Reinforcers _____

Materials _____

Scoring summary:
3—without assistance
2—verbal prompt
1—verbal assistance
0—model and
   explanation

Task statement " ___Complete the step-by-step problem-solving chart___ "

	Dates								
1. Request conference with case manager									
2. Identify present feeling									
3. Identify what happened immediately before incident									
4. Identify what you did immediately after incident									
5. Identify what else you could have done									
6. Select best choice from #5 (at least two possibilities)									
7. Go back to situation and try choice you selected									
8. Report to case manager what happened when you tried it									
9. Identify present feeling about incident									
10. Identify whether or not any further action needs to be taken									
11.									
12.									
13.									
14.									
15.									
16.									
17.									
18.									
19.									
Number of steps scored 3:									

Figure 3.2. Task analysis—Problem solving.

methods: a) watch a master perform, b) perform the task yourself, c) work backward through the task, d) brainstorm, e) break down complex behaviors.

Instructional Program Format

A second method that can be useful to individuals developing instructional programs utilizes a three-column format (shown later in Figure 3.3). In this approach, each skill to be taught is viewed as having three critical elements that define acceptable performance: response, conditions, and criteria. These three elements are the labels that head the three-column format.

Response   The core of each skill is the response, the middle column of the format. Responses should be observable, measurable behaviors. Behaviors should be described by verbs like "to write," "to lift," "to walk," or "to press." Verbs that are not clearly observable should not be used. "To learn," "to discover," "to understand," and "to concentrate" are terms that lack the clarity to be useful since they are not easily defined or measured.

Conditions   In the conditions column (column number one), the stimuli that come before the response are described. The conditions under which a behavior is to take place clearly have an effect upon the difficulty of that behavior. For example, early in training, it is more difficult for most handicapped trainees to stay on-task in the absence of trainer prompts and feedback than when a trainer is present.

Criteria   The third column, criteria, is for measuring behavior. Behavior can be measured in a number of ways. For example, we can count the number of times a response occurs, measure how long it takes for one behavior to occur, measure how many behaviors occur in a fixed period of time, or how closely a behavior resembles a standard. Proficient performance requires individuals to perform tasks quickly as well as accurately. The level of proficiency required for the acceptable performance of a behavior (regardless of how that level is measured) will have an effect upon the difficulty of each skill. For example, it is easier to hand wash six dishes per hour than to hand wash 60. The basic response (dishwashing) has not changed, but when the rate at which the job must be completed is increased, the difficulty of the behavior required is changed.

Behavioral Techniques

The three-column format provides information useful in developing instructional programming that utilizes three common behavioral techniques: shaping, prompting and fading, and chaining.

Shaping   Shaping refers to a procedure in which better and better approximations of the desired behavior are reinforced until the objective is reached. For example, a trainee may be in a program designed to shape length of time at work. Presently, the individual works between 30 and 40 minutes before leaving the work station. The goal is to work for 1 hour 50 minutes (Department of Labor specifies a 10-minute break every 2 hours). A program utilizing a shaping procedure is shown in the three-column format in Figure 3.3.

In this case, the trainer would reinforce any acceptable behavior as described by the steps listed under criteria. Each step is a successively closer approximation to being at the work station for 1 hour 50 minutes.

Prompting and Fading Prompts are used to facilitate the acquisition of new behaviors by creating conditions under which the behavior is likely to occur and by reducing the number of errors in learning. Prompts may be classified as instructor-mediated prompts or object-mediated prompts.

Instructor-Mediated Prompts Instructor-mediated prompts include physical, gestural, verbal, and imitative prompts. An instructor using a physical prompt physically assists the learner in performing the task. For instance, when teaching a trainee to sweep the floor, the instructor may stand behind the client and place his or her hands over the client's hands while the client is holding the broom. It should be noted that the instructor is not doing the task for the trainee. Rather, guidance is being provided that will ultimately be faded out so that the individual performs the entire task independently.

A gestural prompt is one in which the instructor makes a gesture to indicate the correct response. When teaching sweeping, the instructor may point to the broom and to the floor. One common use of gestural prompts is to indicate the correct response when several choices are presented. For example, an instructor who is teaching an individual to choose a red transistor when presented with three additional objects may say, "Sally, pick up the red transistor," and at the same time point to the red transistor.

Verbal prompts refer to verbal instruction. The instructor may tell the janitorial trainee to pick up the broom, how to hold the broom, and how to make a sweeping motion. Imitative prompts are prompts in which the instructor indicates a demonstration is about to occur and then models the correct response.

Condition	Response	Criteria
When the horn sounds	Work	35 minutes
" " " "	"	40 minutes
" " " "	"	45 minutes
" " " "	"	50 minutes
" " " "	"	55 minutes
" " " "	"	60 minutes
" " " "	"	65 minutes
" " " "	"	etc.

Figure 3.3.   Example of a shaping procedure.

Object-Mediated Prompts Object-mediated prompts are cues assigned to an object that assist the individual in performing the desired behavior. The use of color, photographs, or models may serve as object-mediated prompts. For instance, janitors use different spray cleaners for various cleaning jobs such as dusting furniture, cleaning windows, cleaning stainless steel, and disinfecting/cleaning porcelain. If each cleaner is kept in the same style spray bottle, the bottles can be color coded for each job so that "yellow is for dusting," "blue is for the windows," etc. Photographs, self-recording, and praise were used by Connis (1979) to increase independent task changes by four moderately retarded individuals in a vocational training program. Independent task changes were defined as beginning a new task without instructions. The procedure consisted of posting photographs of the tasks in correct sequence on a wall in each individual's work area. Below each picture was a blank paper. Each individual was taught to walk to the photographs, look at the appropriate photo in the sequence, mark an "X" on the blank paper, and begin the task represented in the photo within the 40-second time limit. Sowers, Rusch, Connis, and Cummings (1980) and Johnson and Cuvo (1981) have also demonstrated the effectiveness of pictorial cues in teaching various complex behaviors.

Fading Fading is the gradual removal of prompts. Generally, most prompts are used to exert temporary control over the behavior, and eventually the learner performs the behavior without the prompt. This is done by fading. In most cases, prompts are faded by first removing those that require the most staff assistance (physical prompt) and then removing those that require less staff assistance (verbal prompt). Figure 3.4 shows an example of a procedure for the gradual removal of prompts. Notice that the response and criteria are held constant as the stimulus is changed.

Chaining When discrete behaviors are combined to form complex behaviors, the process is referred to as chaining. For example, after we have shaped time at work station as show in Figure 3.3, we may then add getting own work, starting on time, and putting work away at the end of the day. These are all behaviors that comprise the complex chain called "work."

There are three approaches utilized in teaching the complex components of a behavior: forward chaining, backward chaining, and whole task training. In forward chaining, the instructor begins by teaching the first step of the task analysis and adding subsequent steps as each previous step is mastered. For example, to forward chain a task consisting of five steps, you would teach step one, then teach steps one and two, followed by steps one, two, and three until all five steps had been taught. Backward chaining refers to a procedure in which the final step of the task is taught first and preceding steps are gradually added. To backward chain our five-step task, you would first teach step five, then steps four and five, then steps three, four, and five until all five steps had been learned. In whole task training, all steps of the task are taught in a sequence from beginning to end during each training session. For example, whole task

Condition	Response	Criteria
1. Given a dirty floor, gestural and verbal prompt	Place mop head into wringer on mop bucket	Five of five trials on three consecutive days
2. Given dirty floor and a verbal prompt	Same as above	Same as above
3. Given a dirty floor	Same as above	Same as above

Figure 3.4. Example of a fading procedure.

training of the five-step task would consist of repeatedly teaching steps one, two, three, four, and five until the whole task is learned. There are no set guidelines for when to use forward chaining, backward chaining, or whole task training. Which method you choose depends on the task (tasks like swimming cannot be backward chained), the learner, and the trainer (use procedures you have had success with in the past).

Exercise

3-6. Identify at least one programming technique that may be effective in teaching each of the following vocational skills: a) discriminating between drain opener and toilet bowl cleaner, b) cutting the lawn in front of the factory in less than 2 hours, c) assembling ball point pens.

Answer to Exercise

3-6. a) fading
     b) shaping
     c) chaining

SUGGESTED ACTIVITIES

1. Examine your training curriculum. How many of the skills taught are critical skills? Questions that may be useful are: How would you redesign your curriculum so that only critical skills are taught? Are these skills prerequisite skills for future skills or are they "busy time" skills? If trainees cannot perform this skill, what effect might this have on their vocational survival?
2. Identify one local job. Create a list of valid activities within that job. Do a careful task analysis of *one* of those activities.

REFERENCES

Baer, D. M. The control of the developmental process: Why wait? In: J. R. Nesselroade & H. R. Reese (eds.), *Lifespan developmental psychology*. New York: Academic Press, 1973.

Bellamy, G. T., & Wilcox, B. Secondary education for severely handicapped students: Guidelines for quality services. In: K. P. Lynch, W. E. Kienan, & J. A. Stark (eds.), *Prevocational and vocational education for special needs youth: A Blueprint for the 1980s* Baltimore: Paul H. Brookes Publishing Co., 1982.

Bernstein, G. S. On selecting target behaviors: How many ways are there to get where we're going? *Division 25 Recorder,* 1981, *16,* 7.

Bernstein, G. S., Ziarnik, J. P., Rudrud, E. H., Czajkowski, L. A. *Behavioral habilitation through proactive programming.* Baltimore: Paul H. Brookes Publishing Co., 1981.

Brown, L., Branston, M. B., Hamre-Nietupski, S., Pumpian, I., Certo, N., & Gruenewald, L. A strategy for developing chronological age-appropriate and functional curricular content for severely handicapped adolescents and young adults. *The Journal of Special Education,* 1979, *13,* 81–90.

Brown, L., Pumpian, I., Baumgart, P., Vandeventer, P., Ford, A., Nisbet, J., Schroeder, J., & Gruenewald, L. Longitudinal transition plans in programs for severely handicapped children. *Exceptional Children,* 1981, *47,* 624–630.

Connis, R. T. The effect of the sequential pictorial cues, self-recording, and praise on the job task sequencing of retarded adults. *Journal of Applied Behavior Analysis,* 1979, *12,* 355–361.

Fredericks, H. D. B., Anderson, R. B., Baldwin, V. L., Grove, D., Moore, W. G., Moore, M., & Beaird, J. H. *The identification of competencies of teachers of the severely handicapped.* Monmouth, OR: Teaching Research Division, 1977.

Johnson, B. F., & Cuvo, J. J. Teaching mentally retarded adults to cook. *Behavior Modification,* 1981, *5,* 187–202.

Moyer, J. R., & Dardig, J. C. Practical task analysis for special educators. *Teaching Exceptional Children,* 1978, *11,* 16–18.

Rudrud, E., Ferrara, J., Wendelgass, P., Markve, R. A., & Decker, D. Community-referenced procedures for informing developmentally disabled clients about occupational training options. *Vocational Evaluation and Work Adjustment Bulletin,* 1982, *15,* 89–93.

Sowers, J. A., Rusch, F. R., Connis, R. G., & Cummings, L. V. Teaching mentally retarded adults to time manage in a vocational setting. *Journal of Applied Behavior Analysis,* 1980, *13,* 119–128.

Wehman, P. Help wanted: New approaches to unemployment. *TASH Newsletter,* 1983, *9*(4), 1–2.

Wilcox, B., & Bellamy, G. T. *Design of high school programs for severely handicapped students.* Baltimore: Paul H. Brookes Publishing Co., 1982.

Ziarnik, J. P. Preparing mentally retarded adolescents for societal adaptation. In: N. Anastasiow (ed.), *New directions for exceptional children* (No. 5). San Francisco: Jossey-Bass, 1981.

Unit II

SERVICE DELIVERY ISSUES

CHAPTER 4

Service Delivery Models

OBJECTIVES

To be able to:
1. Describe the differences between the continuum of services and the array of services models.
2. Discuss the potential advantages and disadvantages of the continuum of services model.
3. Discuss the potential advantages and disadvantages of the array of services model.

The purpose of this chapter is to familiarize the reader with two different models of service delivery: the continuum model and the array model. This chapter presents what we believe are the advantages and disadvantages of each. As you read, you must be prepared to critically evaluate the advantages and drawbacks of the model around which your agency or program is organized.

SERVICE CONTINUUM MODEL

The basis for the continuum model of service delivery is related to the belief that individuals change and grow (i.e., develop) throughout their lives, and that, in order to be comprehensive, services need to accommodate these changes (Johnson, 1982; Schulman, 1980). According to the President's Panel on Mental Retardation (1962), the comprehensive continuum describes the selection, blending, and use, in proper sequence and relationship, of the medical, educational, and social services required by a retarded person to minimize his disability at every point in his life span . . . . A continuum of care permits fluidity of movement of the individual from one type of service to another.

The continuum notion has been most frequently translated into a model in which program services decrease in frequency and intensity as the person approaches independence. In the continuum, the individual moves from one service to the next. Figure 4.1 illustrates this model. As you can see, minimum independence is associated with maximum program services, while maximum independence is associated with minimum program services. Figure 4.2 shows the model described in terms of vocational services (e.g., DuRand & Neufeldt, 1980; Kiernan, 1979; Parker, Taylor, Hartman, Wong, Gregg, & Shay, 1976). While maximum program services are provided to persons who are least independent, these services are generally delivered in the most restrictive and segregated environments. Conversely, maximum independence is associated with minimum program services in the least restrictive and most integrated setting.

The services that make up this continuum in vocational settings can be described as follows:

1. *Extended evaluation and training programs.* Though often viewed as long-term, extended evaluation and training programs can be transitional in nature. Services are usually provided in some centralized location for the purposes of evaluation and work training. Services are often sub-

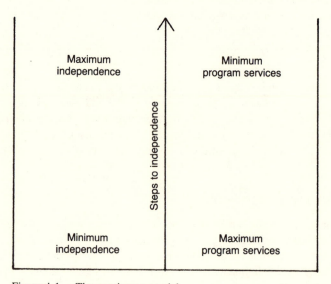

Figure 4.1.   The continuum model.

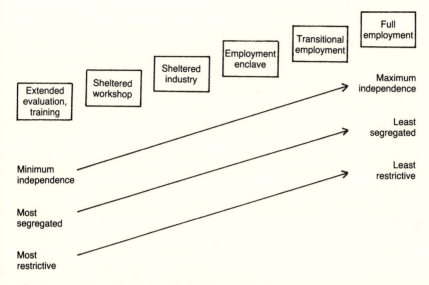

Figure 4.2. The continuum of vocational services.

divided into activity center, work activities, and work adjustment. Emphasis is placed on the development of skills that lead to vocational independence, often in the absence of productive work.

2. *Sheltered workshop.* In sheltered workshops, persons who for whatever reasons have yet to obtain competitive employment perform subsidized work for pay in a controlled environment. Sheltered workshops can be long- or short-term placements in which subsidized work is intended to prepare an individual for competitive work.

3. *Sheltered industry.* Sheltered industry is profit and production oriented, providing sheltered employment to persons earning minimum wage or better. While the work force is comprised largely of individuals with handicaps, there may be a few nonhandicapped workers as well.

4. *Employment enclave.* A small work force of handicapped persons work in a business that employs a majority of nonhandicapped workers. Though the range of tasks is unlimited (e.g., janitorial, subassembly, food service), the enclave remains separate from the rest of the regular business. Pay is performance based and handicapped persons are expected to perform work tasks as well as nonhandicapped individuals.

5. *Transitional employment.* Transitional employment includes all categories of subsidized training in which a disabled worker is fully integrated into a regular job setting. Trainees are employed in this setting for a limited period of time to adjust to the work tasks prior to gaining full employment. On the job training (OJT) would be included here.

6. *Full competitive employment.* Full competitive employment means that an individual works at a regular job with no program support beyond what any worker usually receives.

Possible Advantages of the Continuum

When reviewing the continuum, you must be aware that not all of the advantages or disadvantages we have noted are empirically based. Also, try to think of the possible benefits or disadvantages from the client's perspective. That, of course, should be a major point of reference for all programmatic judgments. Please critically think for yourself as you review both the benefits and disadvantages of the continuum of services.

Instructor Efficiency   Working with a group of persons (5–20) in one place can make it easier for an instructor to interact daily with each person. Remember that movement along the continuum is defined by individual level of independence. Thus, as persons enter vocational sites where they are more dispersed and integrated, they should need less instructor interaction, which is less convenient to deliver anyway under these conditions. It is easier to train and monitor when all trainees are in one 10' × 25' room.

Facilitation of Grouping and Instruction   Persons in more restrictive environments can be easily grouped for instruction on the basis of shared characteristics or service needs. Instructors may need to develop less diverse instructional techniques when working with a group of similar persons.

Logicalness   The continuum is an orderly model that makes sense to most people. It is logical to structure programs so that as trainees develop more independence, they should progress to service sites that provide less intensive programming.

Increased Peer Contact   There is the potential that handicapped persons will increase social interaction and feel less isolated when placed with other handicapped individuals. By forming an easily accessed peer group, the environment is perhaps less threatening than a more integrated environment in which the trainee might encounter less peer acceptance.

Increased Staff Interaction   Staff in a large facility have more opportunities to interact, share ideas, and provide mutual support than do staff who are dispersed. One major problem that we encounter with staff who provide programs to trainees at dispersed sites is feelings of isolation. Even attending a weekly staff meeting is seldom sufficient to help dispersed staff feel less isolated.

Administrative Efficiency   Staff supervision and program management are easier if staff and programs are less dispersed and more centrally located. For example, staff absences are more easily covered if one staff is removed from a group of four than if a single staff at a dispersed site is absent. Billing and central records are also facilitated.

Decreased Expenses   The continuum of services model is less expensive because it takes fewer staff, less duplication of materials, fewer transportation costs, and less liability insurance to provide services in one place.

Possible Disadvantages of the Continuum

Decreased Involvement with Nonhandicapped Persons   The majority of people in the continuum are served in sheltered workshops or in extended evaluation/training programs (Greenleigh Associates, Inc. 1975) and seldom move along the continuum (U.S. Department of Labor, 1979). Thus, while the continuum does offer service sites where there is interaction with nonhandicapped persons, few handicapped persons will be able to take advantage of them. With only handicapped persons as peers, trainees will not have the opportunity to witness and experience adaptive age-appropriate behavior. Additionally, there is evidence to suggest that staff, without normal models, begin to tolerate and perhaps even reinforce increasing amounts of deviance from clients (Certo, Belmore, Crowner, & Brown, 1976). Therefore, when considering realistic expectations for trainees, attention needs to be given to both the importance society places on the behavior (Kazdin, 1977; Wolf, 1978) and whether the goal accurately reflects society's standards for how people generally behave (Voeltz & Evans, 1983).

Example 4.1.

Staff tolerance for deviant behaviors is both subtle and varied. How many of the following situations do you recognize? How many more can you think of?
1. In the lunch room, a client spilled his milk. Staff responded with a verbal reprimand to be more careful and a command to clean up the milk. Later that afternoon, during a break, a staff person spilled a soda. Staff responded with good-natured teasing and helped with cleaning.
2. A staff person went to ask a question of her supervisor, whom she found talking to a parent. She waited politely until the supervisor paused and acknowledged her, whereupon she made her request. A few minutes later, a client, without waiting to be acknowledged, asked a question of the supervisor, who interrupted his talk with the parent to answer.
3. The staff person who is habitually late returning from breaks and lunches comments, "We need to teach clients to be 100% on time so they can survive on jobs."

Necessity for Retraining Skills   There is no reason to believe that skill independence exhibited at one level in the continuum will be exhibited at the next level in a dissimilar environment. Any skill generalization across settings must be explicitly trained. Therefore, retraining of skills may be necessary when the individual changes environments.

Increased Overall Costs   While costs of day vocational programs vary from state to state, it is undeniable that the costs add up for each year that a person remains in training.

Analysis

The determination of the ultimate worth of any service model must involve an analysis of the costs involved in achieving goals and the frequency with which goals are achieved. The often-stated goal of the continuum of services as presently practiced is to prepare disabled individuals for independent function-ing in competitive jobs (Bellamy, Rhodes, Bourbeau, & Mank, 1982). When evaluating the worth of the continuum model, the following facts must be considered:

1. Annual likelihood of placement for individuals who have been in work-shop programs longer than 2 years is 3% (Moss, 1979).
2. Movement within the continuum (e.g., from work activities to regular work programs) seems to average around 3% annually (California De-partment of Finance, 1979; U.S. Department of Labor, 1979).
3. Based on these movement data, mentally retarded individuals in adult day programs would average between 47 and 58 years to move through the continuum into employment (Bellamy et al., in press).
4. Handicapped persons in all types of programs across the continuum earn an average of 80¢ per hour (U.S. Department of Labor, 1979).
5. Individuals with borderline intelligence (IQ 70–85) comprise the largest proportion of persons in sheltered workshops (Greenleigh Associates, Inc., 1975). Generally, individuals with less severe problems require less behavior training than more severely impaired persons (Walls, Tseng, & Zarin, 1976). Thus, the poor movement and placement data presently available are based upon individuals who ought to be easiest to train (Bellamy et al., in press).
6. Schneider, Rusch, Henderson, and Geske (1981) analyzed cost of em-ployment training versus cost of maintenance in sheltered work and concluded that the costs of employment training were recovered within 2 years of successful placement, while sheltered workshops always operated at a cost.

These findings lead to the conclusion that, as presently practiced, move-ment through a continuum of services is virtually nonexistent. If cost-effective achievement of outcomes (i.e., client movement and employment) is the goal of the vocational continuum, that model must be termed a dismal failure.

THE ARRAY OF SERVICES MODEL

An alternative to the continuum of services is a model in which an individual's independence is not related to where and how services are delivered. This model is called the array (Johnson, 1982) or counselor directed (Wehman & Hill, 1982) model. In this model, as in the continuum, employment is the final goal. However, unlike the continuum, services are always provided in the least restrictive, most integrated setting possible, regardless of the level of client independence. This array of services model can be conceptualized as shown in Figure 4.3 or, may be seen from the client's perspective as shown in Figure 4.4.

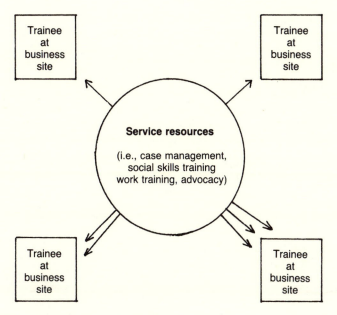

Figure 4.3.   The array of services model.

This model can deliver the same services as the continuum and account for the changing needs of people, but does so in a different way than the service continuum. In the service array model, the person is placed into an existing business or industrial site and receives needed services in that job environment. Various support services are arranged to allow the person to function in the least restrictive, most integrated environment. That is, whatever services necessary to allow a person to maintain his or her job are delivered on-site. If the trainee needs to learn to be on-task, the trainer works with that person at the job site to increase on-task behavior. If money management is an issue, the trainee is taught how to handle money on the job, such as buying lunch or using vending machines. As the person's needs change, services can be added, reduced, or eliminated.

Example 4.2.

Wehman and Hill (1982) describe a program in which 56 clients were placed into competitive jobs over a 3-year period. One year follow-up data indicated that 35 of the persons were still employed. Clients were, for the most part, moderately retarded ($N = 29$), and 21 of the individuals had multiple handicaps. Job sites were diverse, ranging from food service and janitorial to assembly. Wehman and Hill (1982) believe that job placement is the primary habilitation goal of vocational services (as opposed to the more general goal of client independence). In this program, staff spend considerable time identifying job opportunities, gaining employer commitment to hire a handicapped person, and providing maximum

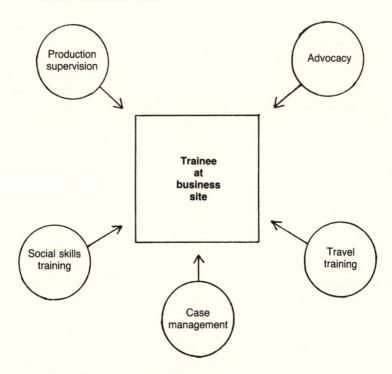

Figure 4.4.   Delivery of an array of vocational services.

intervention to help the trainee remain on the job. They believe that lack of job seeking skills should not necessarily hold a person back from gaining successful employment. The 56 severely disabled persons involved in this project did not have to "progress" through a continuum. They went straight to the job site. Before you object to this approach because 21 out of 56 persons failed to retain their jobs, remember that 35 people did make it! Within the last 3 years, have 62% of all (not just those placed, but *all*) your trainees successfully gained and maintained competitive employment?

Potential Advantages

Potential advantages of the array of services model are described below.

Increased Exposure to Nonhandicapped Persons   Because the handi-capped individual is served in an existing business or industrial setting, there are numerous nonhandicapped models with which to interact. The opportunity to see appropriate work and social behaviors, to receive social consequences for adaptive and maladaptive behaviors, and to have to respond to the demands of an integrated nonsheltered workplace produce numerous positive changes in trainees.

Reduction of Generalization Problems   One cannot expect skill generalization from one training site to another. The array of services model completely bypasses this problem by teaching needed vocational skills in the environment(s) where they must be exhibited.

Positive Community-Employer Attitudes Virtually all programs that have utilized the array of services approach have reported positive changes in community and employer attitudes toward handicapped persons. Brickey and Campbell (1981) noted the positive attitudes of nonhandicapped employees and the helpfulness of supervisors. Certo et al. (1976) reported how initial employer reluctance turned into enthusiasm after program success. We have seen similar effects from our program at Goodwill Industries of Denver, where one company president wrote his branch managers nationwide to urge them to become involved after the success of the Denver project.

Increased Independent Client Performance Many of the poor work behaviors exhibited in segregated work or training programs are a function of the characteristics of the environment rather than of the client per se. For example, in many segregated settings, trainees are taught to work until a task is done or materials exhausted and then wait for further instructions. At a regular worksite, this is rarely the case. Rather, workers must pace themselves throughout a day and often need to independently initiate getting replacement materials or otherwise remain busy. Another behavior that is a function of a segregated environment is trainee dependence on staff presence as a cue for appropriate behavior. In business sites, trainees become increasingly reliant on a variety of nonstaff cues for appropriate behavior, such as nonhandicapped co-workers.

Improved Staff/Client Morale Morale increases when staff and clients have a challenging but visible goal to work toward, and sufficient support to ensure success. Additionally, staff take pride in a program that actually achieves goals on a regular basis.

Reduced Long-Term Program Costs Because of the superior placement success rate of the array model, long-term program costs are greatly reduced (Brickey & Campbell, 1981; Wehman & Hill, 1982). Also, when people are competitively employed, they pay federal and state taxes, and benefits such as Supplemental Security Income (SSI) are reduced.

Potential Disadvantages

Increased Short-Term Expenses Wehman & Hill (1982) report a total program cost of $247,618 for a 3-year program that placed 56 individuals in competitive employment. They estimate day program costs for those same individuals to have been $169,161. Thus, in the short run, the provision of regular day services to those same persons would have been cheaper. Therefore, a real drawback to the array model is that state and federal funding sources are not easily convinced to pay large amounts of money up front, for ultimate savings. Such sources have heard the same argument repeatedly in numerous other situations, so they are wary of promises to save them money.

More Complex Administrative Support   The basic logistics of administration, support services (e.g., secretarial, fiscal), project supervision, coordination of services, and documentation are increased as staff travel to trainees at dispersed sites. Take, for example, supervision. A supervisor must now travel to several remote sites if he or she is interested in gathering first-hand information regarding trainer functions. Similarly, staff travel time and scheduling make it difficult to track down a staff person quickly in the event of an emergency.

Limited Trainee Criteria   None of the reported projects (e.g., Brickey & Campbell, 1981; Wehman & Hill, 1982) really describe entry criteria. While trainee demographics are provided (e.g., age, sex, disability), we are not informed as to who was not selected and why. We do know (e.g., Wehman & Hill, 1982) that as severity of cognitive impairment increases, success in job maintenance seems to decrease. However, the number of trainees served is so small that this conclusion is tentative at best and perhaps signifies a need for intensified follow-along or work with residential providers. Certo et al. (1976) reported that placing an obviously impaired individual on the job resulted in such overwhelming resentment from nonhandicapped persons performing the same job that some training of complex job skills had to be done prior to the trainee entering the job site. At our program in Denver, we have a number of minimal entry criteria for the array model aspect of our program including regular attendance, low rate of major maladaptive behaviors such as physical assault, independence in personal care such as eating and toileting, and mobility (the individual does not necessarily have to be ambulatory). Thus, immediate placement in a job environment might not be feasible for all trainees.

More Complex Program Delivery   Staff must be well organized. Because they are traveling to clients, they must anticipate any program needs prior to arriving at the job site. If a data sheet or stopwatch is forgotten, it is impossible to take a minute and go to the office and get it. Further, any communication difficulties seem even worse in the array of services model. Scheduling, communication networks, and staff cooperation/coordination are critical if the model is to be maximally effective.

Analysis

The goal of the array of services model, like the continuum, is to enable individuals to function independently in competitive jobs. The difference, as pointed out earlier, is that the array of services model does not require individual independence as a prerequisite for placement, rather it is gained as a result of placement. Admittedly, the array model has seldom been utilized outside of special demonstration projects. However, it does hold considerable promise. When evaluating the worth of the array of services model, consider the following facts:

1. Wehman and Hill (1982) maintained 35 of 56 persons with severe handicaps in competitive employment. Brickey and Campbell (1981) report 13 of 17 persons were still employed at a follow-up 1 year later.
2. The majority of persons with whom the array model has been utilized have been diagnosed as being moderately retarded. This means the model has been effective with persons who are more impaired than the majority of persons presently in sheltered employment.
3. The higher initial costs of placement via the array model are quickly recovered through the reduction of program costs and individual benefits and through taxes paid by the worker (Schneider et al., 1981; Wehman & Hill, 1982).

CONCLUSIONS

There is little doubt that we must seriously consider major alterations in current models of delivering vocational habilitation services. However, the solutions are decidedly complex, involving all the social, political, and fiscal factors encountered in any large-scale change. Unfortunately, declaring a need for reform in the way services are structured is not particularly helpful to the individual trainer, program manager, or even an agency director who has immediate responsibilities for service provision but is unlikely to be in a position to devote extensive efforts to system change. However, considerable change can occur at the individual program level.

Bernstein and Karan (1979) noted a number of obstacles that keep trainees from attaining vocational independence. Many of these are open to manipulation by agency staff and are a focus of several chapters in this book including questionable evaluation practices, a lack of program definition (e.g., trying to be all things to all people), a lack of incentives for developing age-appropriate work skills, overprotectiveness by caretakers, and a lack of program accountability. All of these factors can be addressed by individual agencies without having to wait for the reform of an entire system.

We believe that, whatever changes are made in the delivery of vocational services, the single most critical item that will produce change is the establishment of quality maintenance and evaluation procedures that are oriented to both *product* (What did we do? e.g., wages earned, individual objectives achieved, individuals successfully employed) and *process* (How well did we do it? e.g., ratings of staff quality, difficulty of objectives, individual program quality; Did anybody care? e.g., social validation outcomes) (Bernstein, 1983).

The remainder of this book should give you many ideas and strategies for altering the manner in which vocational training services are delivered.

REFERENCES

Bellamy, G. T., Rhodes, L. E., Bourbeau, P. E., & Mank, D. M. *Mental retardation services in sheltered workshops and day activity programs: Consumer outcomes and policy alternatives.* Paper presented at the National Working Conference on Vocational Services and Employment Opportunities, Madison, Wisconsin, 1982.

Bernstein, G. S. System maintenance: Behavioral quality control. In: J. P. Ziarnik (Chair), *Disseminating behavioral technology: Program engineering in a vocational training agency.* Group poster session presented at the meeting of the Association for Behavior Analysis, Milwaukee, May, 1983.

Bernstein, G. S., & Karan, O. C. Obstacles to vocational normalization for the developmentally disabled. *Rehabilitation Literature,* 1979, *40*(3), 66–71.

Brickey, M., & Campbell, K. Fast food employment for moderately and mildly mentally retarded adults: The McDonald's project. *Mental Retardation,* 1981, *19*(3), 113–116.

California Department of Finance. *A review of sheltered workshops and related programs (Phase II): To assemble concurrent resolution* (Vol. II, No. 206). Final report to the State of California, Sacramento, 1979.

Certo, N., Belmore, K., Crowner, T., & Brown, L. A review of secondary level educational service delivery models for severely handicapped students. In: L. Brown, N. Certo, K. Belmore, & J. Crowner (eds.), *Madison's alternative for zero exclusion: Papers and programs related to public school services for secondary age severely handicapped students* (Vol. VI). Madison, WI: Madison Public Schools, 1976.

DuRand, J., & Neufeldt, A. H. Comprehensive vocational services. In: R. Flynn & K. Nitsch (eds.), *Normalization, social integration, and community services.* Baltimore: University Park Press, 1980.

Greenleigh Associates, Inc. *The role of the sheltered workshop in the rehabilitation of the severely handicapped.* Report to the U.S. Department of Health, Education, and Welfare, Rehabilitation Services Administration, New York, NY, 1975.

Johnson, T. *A report of the assessment of four residential programs for adults with developmental disabilities.* Clintonville, WI: Central Office of Unified Health Services of Shawano/Waupaca Counties, 1982.

Kazdin, A. E. Assessing the clinical or applied importance of behavior change through social validation. *Behavior Modification,* 1977, *1*, 427–452.

Kiernan, W. Rehabilitation planning. In: P. R. Magrab & J. O. Elder (eds.), *Planning for services to handicapped persons: Community, education, health.* Baltimore: Paul H. Brookes Publishing Co., 1979.

Moss, J. W. *Post secondary vocational education for mentally retarded adults.* Final report to the division of Developmental Disabilities, Rehabilitation Services Administration, U.S. Department of Health, Education, and Welfare, 1979. (Grant No. 56P 50281/0)

Parker, S. L., Taylor, G., Hartman, W., Wong, R., Gregg, D., & Shay, D. *Improving occupational programs for the handicapped.* Washington, DC: U.S. Department of Health, Education, and Welfare, 1976.

President's Panel on Mental Retardation. *A proposed program for national action to combat mental retardation.* Washington, DC: U.S. Government Printing Office, 1962.

Schneider, K., Rusch, F. R., Henderson, R., & Geske, T. *Competitive employment for mentally retarded persons: Costs versus benefits.* Unpublished manuscript, Department of Special Education, University of Illinois, Champaign, 1981.

Schulman, E. D. *Focus on the retarded adult.* St. Louis: C. V. Mosby Co., 1980.

U.S. Department of Labor. *Study of handicapped clients in sheltered workshops* (Vol. II). Washington, DC: U.S. Department of Labor, 1979.

Voeltz, L. M., & Evans, I. M. Educational validity: Procedures to evaluate outcomes in programs for severely handicapped learners. *Journal of the Association for the Severely Handicapped,* 1983, *8*(1), 3–15.

Walls, R., Tseng, M., & Zarin, H. Time and money for clients with mild, moderate, and severe retardation. *American Journal of Mental Deficiency,* 1976, *80*(6), 595–601.

Wehman, P., & Hill, M. *Vocational training and placement of severely disabled persons: Project employability* (Vol. III). Richmond: School of Education, Virginia Commonwealth University, 1982.

Wolf, M. M. Social validity: The case for subjective measurement, or how applied behavior analysis is finding its heart. *Journal of Applied Behavior Analysis,* 1978, *11*, 203–214.

CHAPTER 5

Toward Competitive Employment

OBJECTIVES

To be able to:
1. Describe instructional advances that have contributed to models of training for competitive employment.
2. Describe three models of training for competitive employment: generic, targeted, and on-site training.
3. Describe the common elements found in successful employment training programs.

The purpose of this chapter is to familiarize you with three of the more commonly utilized vocational models for achieving competitive employment, to describe differences between the models, and to describe elements common to each. This chapter will not extensively review programs that have demonstrated circumscribed skill acquisition in sheltered employment settings (e.g., Gold & Barclay, 1973; O'Neill & Bellamy, 1978; Renzaglia, Wehman, Schutz, & Karan, 1976) or review programs that have demonstrated job skill acquisition without placement (e.g., Cuvo, Leaf, & Borakove, 1978). Rather, we are interested in reviewing programs that have tested a complete set of procedures for job development, competitive placement, and maintenance in competitive employment. This is not to deny the value of programs demonstrating job skill acquisition in sheltered employment. In fact, most of what this book is about has been made possible by pioneer work in the areas of job skill acquisition, social skills training, and promotion of maintenance and generalization that took place in sheltered settings.

The development of applications of behavioral technology to competitive employment parallels similar applications in other fields such as child behavior. Principles developed in laboratory settings were tested and refined in narrow, controlled environments such as institutions before being applied in broader, less controlled environments such as the community (Peterson, 1967).

JOB SKILL ACQUISITION

Recent advances in instructional technology (e.g., Bellamy, Horner, & Inman, 1979; Gold, 1972; Karan, Wehman, Renzaglia, & Schutz, 1976) have opened the doors to exciting new vocational worlds by questioning the limits of who and what we can teach. One need not look too far in books and journals to find numerous demonstrations of successful acquisition of complex vocational skills by individuals who previously were considered impossible to teach. Thus, programs are no longer limited to utilizing simple work tasks; rather, programs can now teach trainees to perform any work that is available (Crosson, 1969). For example, mentally retarded persons have been taught to master a variety of assembly tasks including a 19-piece cam switch actuator (Bellamy, Peterson, & Close, 1975) and a 79-step Tektronix cable harness (Hunter & Bellamy, 1976).

Consider the following example. Hunter and Bellamy (1976) taught three persons with severe mental retardation to assemble a cable harness for use in oscilloscopes. Assembly involved 79 separate steps. Trainee I was a 20-year-old woman with Down's syndrome who had been institutionalized for the previous 16 years. She obtained a Stanford-Binet Mental Age of 2.6 years and a Vineland Social Maturity Scale quotient of 2.5 years. Trainee II was a 26-year-old woman with Down's syndrome who had been institutionalized for 23 years and records indicated an assessed IQ of 14. Trainee III was a 19-year-old severely retarded woman who had some previous experience in small parts assembly. All trainees were taught to assemble the cable harness in a forward chain with verbal prompts, modeling, and reinforcement. Incorrect responses were corrected by backing up to a previous successful step and modeling, and verbally prompting to correct the error. Success was defined as five consecutive, error-free assemblies. Trainee I achieved criterion after 72 hours of training during 49 work days. Trainee II achieved criterion in 35 hours (111 minutes per day over 29 days), while Trainee III met criteria in only 18 hours of training.

SOCIAL SKILLS TRAINING

Authors addressing competitive employment (e.g., Rusch & Mithaug, 1980; Wehman, 1981) are unanimous in acknowledging the importance of social skills in gaining and maintaining competitive employment. As we showed in Chapter 2, social/emotional factors are major reasons for mentally retarded persons failing to maintain employment. Unfortunately, as Bernstein (1981) noted, "While the literature on assessing interpersonal skills is confusing and incomplete, the literature on teaching those skills is virtually non-existent" (p. 73). This is in large part a result of demonstrating acquisition of vocational skills in sheltered settings where social skills are not so important. For example, Mithaug and Haring (1977) surveyed sheltered workshop supervisors and found that social skills were generally rated less important relative to other work skills such as on-time, learning new tasks, on-task, and working independently. However, the successes demonstrated in teaching work skills have made us confident that we can teach social skills as well, and some examples of social skill training are beginning to appear in the vocational training literature.

Consider the following example. Bradlyn, Himadi, Crimmins, Christoff, Graves, and Kelly (1983) utilized a group setting to teach conversational skills to five mentally retarded adolescents. The trainees were between 14 and 18 years of age and had IQ scores ranging from 32 to 50. Four conversational skills were targeted for training: question asking, self-disclosure, reinforcing/acknowledging comments, and high interest statements. High interest statements (e.g., activities occurring at school, friends, movies, social events, and television shows) were identified by surveying nonhandicapped adolescents at a local high school. Pretraining assessment, based on five 8-minute samples of each trainee in a conversational setting, indicated that while trainees frequently asked questions, they rarely self-disclosed, and almost never reinforced or talked about high interest topics. Three 20-minute training sessions were conducted weekly, and included modeling by the instructor and trainee rehearsal, followed by feedback on the correctness of the rehearsal. After trainees successfully learned the target behaviors, conversational training was generalized to nonhandicapped peers.

MAINTENANCE AND GENERALIZATION

The definitive conceptual analysis of maintenance and generalization was authored in 1977 by Trevor Stokes and Don Baer. In the article, the authors effectively argue for the development of a technology for producing generalization. However, while the need for such a technology is widely acknowledged, the specific training techniques that produce generalization are still being developed. Studies of applications of procedures designed to maintain and generalize the vocational and social skills of persons with developmental disabilities have been conducted on a number of diverse skills such as generalized language (Anderson & Spradlin, 1980), bus riding skills (Neef, Iwata, & Page, 1978), hand tool use (Walls, Sienicki, & Crist, 1981), and janitorial skills (Cuvo et al., 1978).

Consider the following examples. Rudrud, Ziarnik, and Coleman (in press) reported on the successful reduction of tongue protrusion in a 24-year-old moderately retarded woman with Down's syndrome. The tongue protrusion was unsightly and could potentially limit integration in competitive employment situations. The trainee was taught to reliably discriminate "tongue in" from "tongue out" and to self-record tongue in/out in five half-hour sessions. Training was then extended to the work floor and the client was provided with a series of six 30-minute audio cassette tapes with decreasing numbers of beep tones that served to cue her to self-record tongue in/out. Tongue protrusion was reduced from a baseline of 95% to 0% of observed intervals during intervention. This reduction in tongue protrusion was maintained at a follow-up 3 weeks later when the self-recording procedures were gradually faded and withdrawn.

Horner (1981) reported on the successful generalization of upright walking posture in a 28-year-old severely retarded male. Training in upright walking occurred in a specified area utilizing a radio attached to the trainee that went on when the trainee walked upright and went off when he leaned forward more than 7° from vertical. Once trained, other walking conditions (e.g., to and from work) were simulated by having the trainee walk with peers. Gradually, the radio volume was reduced and, subsequently, the radio was removed. Follow-ups at 7 weeks and 5 months indicated that upright walking had successfully generalized to nontraining settings.

Advances in these areas have been largely responsible for enabling us to consider competitive employment as a realistic outcome for most mentally retarded persons. While it is entirely possible that the number of available community job openings may ultimately limit the number of persons able to gain competitive employment, we believe this is an insufficient reason for limiting training outcomes to anything less than competitive employment in all but the most extreme cases. This idea stems from the fact that most existing vocational habilitation agencies have not yet developed programs of a quality sufficient to test the resources of the competitive labor market. Furthermore, the role of vocational habilitation agencies is to provide vocational training, not to question the state of the economy. Would you tell the numbers of people out of work to stop seeking employment because none exists? Probably not. Similarly, you should not limit trainee outcomes. The following are three models that have achieved this outcome with various degrees of success.

GENERIC PRE-EMPLOYMENT AND TRAINING—THE CONTINUUM OF SERVICES MODEL

In February of 1982, Goodwill Industries of Denver contracted with the University of Colorado School of Medicine for supervision of Goodwill's Vocational Services Program under the direction of this book's second and third authors. At that time, a decision was made to retain and improve the continuum of services model currently in place at Goodwill for two reasons. First, state reimbursement for vocational services was so low that the costs of intense on the job training as described by Schutz and Rusch (1982) and Wehman and Hill (1982) could not be met with the usually available funding levels. Second, the continuum is the most widely practiced model in Colorado, and we wanted other practitioners to be able to view a quality program within a model with which they could readily identify.

The program is structured similarly to the continuum described in Figure 4.2. The trainee's present level of behavior is assessed using the Worker Readiness Checklist (Ziarnik, Grupé, Morrison, Cruchon, Conway, & Leeming, 1983). The Checklist was based on the literature on factors related to vocational success reviewed in Chapter 2 and was subsequently socially validated by surveying local employers. In-house programming consists of the acquisition and limited generalization of the 27 generic work skills listed on the Checklist. The complete list of Checklist items is shown in Chapter 9. Training typically occurs in a ratio of one staff member to 14 or more trainees. Once trainees independently engage in the generic work behaviors, they move to less supervised, community-based job sites located in actual businesses. The next move is to on-the-job training sites and subsequently to employment. An average of 70 persons are enrolled in the program quarterly with an average age of 33 years. Most are in the moderately to mildly retarded range with multiple handicaps.

Program data from the first year of operation are encouraging (Bernstein, 1983):

1. By the end of the year, 93% of all clients were making behavioral progress toward achieving training objectives.
2. By the end of the year, individual behavior change programs met an average of 95% of all quality standards on a scale developed by Bernstein, Ziarnik, & Rudrud (1982).
3. Between 95%–99% of all behavior change programs were proactive each quarter (i.e., they were designed to teach or maintain behaviors). Thus, just 1%–4% of all behavior change programs quarterly were aimed at decreasing behaviors.
4. Forty-nine trainees progressed to community-based transitional employment between October of 1982 and June of 1983.
5. Of the six persons placed competitively from the program since July of 1982, all six have maintained employment through August of 1983.
6. Overall, 5%–10% of trainees change program status (e.g., from in-house training to transitional employment) quarterly. Overall, 87.5% of these moves maintained during the first 15 months of the program.

TARGETED PRE-EMPLOYMENT TRAINING—
THE COMMUNITY SERVICES MODEL

This model, first outlined by Frank Rusch and Dennis Mithaug (1980) and expanded by their associates (Rusch, Rusch, Menchetti, & Schutz, in press; Schutz & Rusch, 1982), presents a trilogy of activities (survey-train-place) around which to organize services. Within this framework, training focuses on those skills that are identified as necessary for a person entering and maintaining employment. This is accomplished by first surveying local community employers to determine possible community job placements and generic survival skills in those placements (Rusch, Schutz, & Agran, 1982). Thus, any skill or behavior change training received in this model is directly related to what skills the trainee will need in a specific placement.

Schutz and Rusch (1982) present data from implementation of this model at the Community Services Program developed by University of Illinois staff in Champaign, Illinois. Over 3 years, the program served 34 moderately to severely retarded persons between the ages of 19 and 45. Most trainees were employed in sheltered programs prior to entering Community Services. Entry requirements included no physical handicap, correctable sight and hearing, minimum 18 years of age and 5'2" tall, and no uncontrolled seizures. Training was provided in food service and professional housekeeping in two phases: a) pre-employment, and b) employment. During the pre-employment phase, trainees received training in a 1:3 staff-client ratio on those skills necessary for successful employment in food service or housekeeping. Pre-employment training occurred in ongoing business where specific duties (e.g., kitchen labor) were taken over by Community Services trainees. Thus, from the beginning, vocational training occurred in an environment where trainees were subject to the demands of a work setting and had exposure to numerous nonhandicapped co-workers. However, rather than being competitively employed at this time, trainees were in a sort of sheltered enclave (see Chapter 4). Thus, trainees and trainers had many of the advantages of a competitive job site, with very few of the associated risks. Pre-employment training could last up to 150 days. Once the trainee mastered the identified skills, he or she was then referred for employment training.

The employment training phase secured community job placements, provided on-the-job adjustment training necessary (one day to several weeks depending on trainee needs), and provided follow-along. It is important to note that follow-along was provided indefinitely for all project graduates. Additionally, independent living training was provided during this phase.

Sixty-five percent of all persons referred to Community Services entered and maintained competitive employment. Beyond the obvious trainee benefits such as increased wages and reducton in costs to society (Schneider, Rusch,

Henderson, & Geske, 1981), successful trainees brought stability to typically high turnover positions, so that considerable time and money were saved by employers (Schutz & Rusch, 1982).

INTENSIVE ON-THE-JOB TRAINING— THE ARRAY OF SERVICES MODEL

The array of services model as implemented by Wehman and his colleagues (Wehman, 1981; Wehman & Hill, 1982) was described in Chapter 4. This employment model has also been applied with school populations (Bates & Pancsofar, 1981; Berger, 1983). Berger (1983) reported data for 53 persons ages 18–24 who were placed into a variety of low-tech labor intensive jobs ranging from janitorial and car wash to food service. The majority of individuals had mild ($N = 27$) and borderline ($N = 15$) mental retardation. An 18-month review indicated that 50% of trainees maintained competitive employment.

Common elements of programs that adopt the array of services approach are:

1. Competitive placement, as opposed to the more general goal of vocational independence, is the goal of the program.
2. Services needed to maintain the person in competitive employment are delivered at the job site. Services are gradually withdrawn as the person develops needed skills.
3. Training staff spend considerable time in developing and maintaining relationships with potential employers.
4. Job training is targeted and specific to a single job as opposed to teaching more general generic job skills.
5. Follow-along is provided to help maintain the worker.

COMMON ELEMENTS OF SUCCESSFUL COMPETITIVE EMPLOYMENT PROGRAMS

Use of Behavior Training Strategies

While there are some major differences in trainee population, staff to trainee ratios, and the relative emphasis on the development of generic work skills, all successful competitive employment programs share several common elements. All programs utilize a behavioral approach to service delivery. The behavioral approach (Bernstein, Ziarnik, Rudrud, & Czajkowski, 1981) consists of: a) a focus on specific, observable behaviors, b) a functional analysis of behavior involving identification of controlling antecedents and consequences, and c) a focus on scientifically valid intervention procedures. Additionally, Rusch and

Mithaug (1980) note that the behavioral approach focuses attention on three phases of skill development: acquisition, maintenance, and generalization.

Training Curricula That Have Both Social and Content Validity

Another common element of successful employment training programs is that training areas are researched by asking employers to identify needed skills (e.g., Rusch et al., 1982; Ziarnik, 1983), and by careful task analysis of actual job performance requirements (e.g., Sowers, Thompson, & Connis, 1979). Thus, trainees learn skills identified as necessary for employment.

Targeted Outcomes

While some programs may focus more on the development of generic skills (e.g., Ziarnik, 1983) than others (e.g., Wehman & Hill, 1982), they all train for a specific job or jobs. There are no "shotgun" placements of trainees into jobs that, while they might be available, were not planned for as an integral part of the trainees' skill development.

Follow-Along

All programs provide follow-along. That is, when placed, trainees are not immediately dropped from the program. For example, Schutz and Rusch (1982) note that the Community Services Program provides indefinite follow-along. Goodwill Industries of Denver (Conway, Cruchon, Grupé, Leeming, & Morrison, 1983) provides follow-along that is gradually faded over a 1-year period.

REFERENCES

Anderson, S. R., & Spradlin, J. E. The generalized effects of productive labeling training involving common object classes. *Journal of the Association for the Severely Handicapped*, 1980, *5*(2), 143–157.

Bates, P., & Pancsofar, E. *Project EARN (Employment And Rehabilitation = Normalization): A competitive employment training program for severely disabled youth in the public schools.* Unpublished manuscript, Department of Special Education, Southern Illinois University, Carbondale, 1981.

Bellamy, G. T., Horner, R. H., & Inman, D. *Vocational habilitation of severely retarded adults.* Baltimore: University Park Press, 1979.

Bellamy, G. T., Peterson, L., & Close, D. Habilitation of the severely and profoundly retarded: Illustrations of competence. *Education and Training of the Mentally Retarded*, 1975, *10*, 174–186.

Berger, S. *STETS project report.* Arizona Department of Economic Security, Division of Developmental Disabilities and Mental Retardation Services, District II, Tucson, AZ, 1983.

Bernstein, G. S. Research issues in training interpersonal skills for the mentally retarded. *Education and Training of the Mentally Retarded*, 1981, *16*, 70–74.

Bernstein, G. S. System maintenance: Effective quality control. In: J. P. Ziarnik (Chair), *Disseminating behavioral technology: Program engineering in a vocational training agency.* Group poster session presented at the meeting of the Association for Behavior Analysis, Milwaukee, May, 1983.

Bernstein, G. S., Ziarnik, J. P., & Rudrud, E. H. *Criteria for evaluating change programs.* Unpublished manuscript, University of Colorado Health Sciences Center, Denver, 1982.

Bernstein, G. S., Ziarnik, J. P., Rudrud, E. H., & Czajkowki, L. A. *Behavioral habilitation through proactive programming.* Baltimore: Paul H. Brookes Publishing Co., 1981.

Bradlyn, A. S., Himadi, W. G., Crimmins, D. B., Christoff, K. A., Graves, K. G., & Kelly, J. A. Conversational skills training for retarded adolescents. *Behavior Therapy,* 1983, *14*(2), 314–325.

Conway, K., Cruchon, N., Grupé, R., Leeming, J., & Morrison, C. Program implementation. Constraints of a 1:14 staff ratio. In: J. P. Ziarnik (Chair), *Disseminating behavioral technology: Program engineering in a vocational training agency.* Group poster session presented at the meeting of the Association for Behavior Analysis, Milwaukee, May, 1983.

Crosson, J. A. A technique for programming sheltered workshop environments for training severely retarded workers. *American Journal of Mental Deficiency,* 1969, *73,* 814–818.

Cuvo, A. J., Leaf, R. B., & Borakove, L. S. Teaching janitorial skills to the mentally retarded: Acquisition, generalization, and maintenance. *Journal of Applied Behavior Analysis,* 1978, *11,* 345–355.

Gold, M. W. Stimulus factors in skill training of the retarded on a complex assembly task: Acquisition, transfer, and retention. *American Journal of Mental Deficiency,* 1972, *76,* 517–526.

Gold, M. W., & Barclay, C. R. The learning of difficult visual discriminations by the moderately and severely retarded. *Mental Retardation,* 1973, *11,* 9–11.

Horner, R. H. Stimulus control, transfer, and maintenance of upright walking posture in a severely mentally retarded adult. *American Journal of Mental Deficiency,* 1981, *86*(1), 86–96.

Hunter, J. D., & Bellamy, G. T. Cable harness construction for severely retarded adults: A demonstration of training techniques. In: G. T. Bellamy (ed.), *Habilitation of severely and profoundly retarded adults.* Eugene, OR: Center on Human Development, 1976.

Karan, O. C., Wehman, P., Renzaglia, A., & Schutz, R. *Habilitation practices with the severely developmentally disabled* (Vol. 1). Madison: University of Wisconsin, 1976.

Mithaug, D. E., & Haring, N. G. Community vocational and workshop placement. In: N. G. Haring & L. J. Brown (eds.), *Teaching the severely handicapped,* Vol. II. New York: Grune & Stratton, 1977.

Neef, N. A., Iwata, B. A., & Page, T. J. Public transportation training: In vivo versus classroom instruction. *Journal of Applied Behavior Analysis,* 1978, *11*(3), 331–344.

O'Neill, C. T., & Bellamy, G. T. Evaluation of a procedure for teaching saw-chain assembly to a severely retarded woman. *Mental Retardation,* 1978, *16,* 37–42.

Peterson, R. F. *Expanding the behavior of the laboratory from clinic to home.* Paper presented at the 75th meeting of the American Psychological Association, Washington, DC, September, 1967.

Renzaglia, A., Wehman, P. H., Schutz, R. P., & Karan, O. C. Use of cue redundancy and positive reinforcement to accelerate production in two profoundly retarded workers. In: O. C. Karan, P. Wehman, A. Renzaglia, & R. Schultz (eds.), *Habilitation practices with the severely developmentally disabled* (Vol. 1). Madison: University of Wisconsin, 1976.

Rudrud, E. H., Ziarnik, J. P., & Coleman, G. Reduction of tongue protrusion in a 24-year-old woman with Down's Syndrome through self-monitoring. *American Journal of Mental Deficiency,* in press.

Rusch, F. R., & Mithaug, D. E. *Vocational training for mentally retarded adults: A behavior analytic approach.* Champaign, IL: Research Press, 1980.

Rusch, F. R., Rusch, J. C., Menchetti, B. M., & Schutz, R. P. Survey-train-place: Developing a school-aged vocational curriculum for the severely handicapped student. In: R. DuBose (ed.), *Recommended practices manual for severely handicapped learners.* Springfield: Illinois State Department of Instruction, in press.

Rusch, F. R., Schutz, R. P., & Agran, M. Validating entry-level survival skills for service occupations: Implications for curriculum development. *Journal of the Association for the Severely Handicapped,* 1982, *7*(3), 32–41.

Schneider, K., Rusch, F. R., Henderson, R., & Geske, T. *Competitive employment for mentally retarded persons: Costs versus benefits.* Unpublished manuscript, University of Illinois, Champaign, 1981.

Schutz, R. P., & Rusch, F. R. Competitive employment: Toward employment integration for mentally retarded persons. In: K. P. Lynch, W. E. Kiernan, & J. A. Stark (eds.), *Prevocational and vocational education for special needs youth: A blueprint for the 1980s.* Baltimore: Paul H. Brookes Publishing Co., 1982.

Sowers, J. A., Thompson, L. E., & Connis, R. T. The food service vocational training program. In: G. T. Bellamy, G. O'Connor, & O. C. Karan (eds.), *Vocational rehabilitation of severely handicapped persons.* Baltimore: University Park Press, 1979.

Stokes, T. F., & Baer, D. M. An implicit technology of generalization. *Journal of Applied Behavior Analysis,* 1977, *10,* 349–367.

Walls, R. T., Sienicki, A., & Crist, K. Operations training in vocational skills. *American Journal of Mental Deficiency,* 1981, *85*(4), 360–376.

Wehman, P. *Competitive employment: New horizons for severely disabled individuals.* Baltimore: Paul H. Brookes Publishing Co., 1981.

Wehman, P., & Hill, M. Vocational training and placement of severely disabled persons: Project employability, Vol. III.-1982. Richmond: Virginia Commonwealth University, 1982.

Ziarnik, J. Program development: A design for dissemination. In: J. P. Ziarnik (Chair), *Disseminating behavioral technology: Program engineering in a vocational training agency.* Group poster session presented at the meeting of the Association for Behavior Analysis, Milwaukee, May, 1983.

Ziarnik, J., Grupé, R., Morrison, C., Cruchon, N., Conway, K., & Leeming, J. *Worker Readiness Checklist.* Unpublished manuscript, Goodwill Industries of Denver, 1983.

CHAPTER 6

Secondary School Vocational Training

OBJECTIVES

To be able to:

1. Explain why sending all severely and moderately handicapped secondary school students out of district is inappropriate.

2. List and discuss three programming models for severely handicapped individuals found in the public schools.

3. Explain how community-referenced vocational training may help schools to better serve moderately and severely handicapped students.

4. Outline a procedure for bringing about change in a high school special education program.

5. List three ways in which an adult training facility may assist in the development of a community-referenced secondary school vocational training program.

Staff at vocational facilities often comment that handicapped adolescents coming from high schools seem ill-prepared for the world of work. We believe that vocational training program staff can work with high school teachers to improve this situation. Furthermore, if community training staff were to work directly with high schools helping to develop vocational training programs for handicapped students, it is possible that many students could graduate directly from high school to competitive employment. The purpose of this chapter is to provide background information and suggest some steps that can be taken to develop vocational training programs for high school-aged handicapped students.

THE MISSION OF THE HIGH SCHOOL

In general, the mission of a high school is to provide students with experiences that are likely to enhance their future lives. When students graduate, they should have learned skills that will enable them to lead productive, independent, and satisfying lives. Prior to 1975, the scope of this mission rarely included severely and moderately handicapped children. For them, attendance at local high schools was often out of the question. They were placed in state institutions, sent to special schools, or simply sent home.

When Public Law 94-142 (the Education for All Handicapped Children Act of 1975) was passed, the education of handicapped children suddenly became the responsibility of local schools. Many high school staff were then placed in an unenviable position. Virtually overnight, they were supposed to serve students with whom they had no experience in the absence of materials or useful support services.

Currently, there is a great deal of variability in the way in which different schools attempt to meet the needs of handicapped students. Some schools have made extensive efforts to comply with both the letter and the spirit of PL 94-142. They attempt to teach appropriate objectives in the least restrictive environment possible (Williams, Brown, & Certo, 1975). Other districts have made, at best, half-hearted efforts to meet the needs of these students. In a review of programming in 14 small rural districts, Ferrara, Miller, Monroe, and Thompson (1983) found that, as a rule, moderately and severely handicapped students were sent out of district when they reached high school age. These placements were usually in 24-hour residential settings. Very few situations with this type of placement were viewed as appropriately meeting the individual's needs. Furthermore, one must question whether removing a 14-year-old from his or her home is in the best interest of the student. Most 14-year-olds are ill-prepared to enter the adult world and need the support of family, friends, and community. Handicapped children are no better prepared to leave home than their nonhandicapped peers.

There are individual situations where a student might benefit from an out-of-district placement. However, when a school, as a matter of policy, sends away all severely and moderately handicapped students who are at least 14 years old, we feel that the school is probably failing in its mission.

SERVICE DELIVERY APPROACHES ADOPTED BY SCHOOLS

Sending handicapped students away from the high school was only one of the responses made by schools when they became responsible for the education of all handicapped children. Other responses included extending developmental models to the high school, including moderately and severely handicapped students in academic programs designed for mildly handicapped persons, and work study programs.

Out-of-District Placements

Out-of-district placement is a common approach among small rural school districts. Individuals advocating out-of-district placements generally do so for two reasons. First of all, they suggest that small schools can never provide the facilities and programming that are available outside the district. This same argument has been used to attack small schools in general. While it is true that small districts may never provide the facilities available in bigger districts, being housed in excellent physical facilities does not guarantee excellence in instruction.

Furthermore, taxpayers continue to support small schools. They often feel that most of the advantages that might be gained by busing students to a larger consolidated district would be negated by the social and logistic problems it would create. The existence of local high school programs in a community provides so many advantages to students, their families, and the community in general that busing children long distances to school has not been particularly popular.

The arguments for developing local programming for handicapped students closely parallel those for the existence of small schools themselves. While smaller schools may never provide the facilities for handicapped individuals that are available in larger districts, local facilities and institutions can provide adequate programming. Furthermore, the benefits to students, their families, and the community can be substantial. Students, for example, could be trained to work at jobs in their home community. Parents would not have to make 200-mile trips to visit their children. Finally, when schools serve handicapped learners in their home towns, those students' rights as individual citizens are reaffirmed.

The second reason for sending students outside the district relates to state special education funding rules. School funding rules, in some states, actually penalize districts that provide services for handicapped students in local schools. In South Dakota, for example, the state will reimburse 50% of a school's costs when special education services are provided locally. The state pays 100% of the costs of out-of-district placements. It is naive to think that this sort of funding situation will not influence administrative decisions about providing local programs.

In spite of the obstacles to program development, there are data that suggest that fewer schools are sending students out of district. The percentage of persons in residential facilities who entered between the age of 0 and 19 fell from 88% in 1965 to 65% in 1977 (Lakin, Hill, Hauber, & Bruininks, 1982). If this trend continues, in the next few years, the number of school-aged students in residential facilities will be further reduced.

Developmental Model Programs

Curricula built upon developmental models are employed in some programs. The disadvantages of the developmental model have been described in Chapter 2 and will not be repeated here. However, Example 6.1 is included to demonstrate that when secondary school programs are based on the developmental model, teachers are actively training 18-year-olds to behave like 5-year-olds.

Example 6.1.

A Truly Developmental Teacher

Teacher: "It's really true!"
Consultant: "What's that?"
Teacher: "These students I teach are 'forever children!' They behave just like preschoolers."
Consultant: "What do you use for a curriculum?"
Teacher: "Love and hugs."
Consultant: "I mean, what goals and objectives do you use?"
Teacher: "Oh, *that* curriculum. I just get their mental ages from the psychologist then I look up an age-appropriate behavior in that green preschool book over there."
Consultant: "Is this working well for you?"
Teacher: "Sometimes it is trying, but there are rewards. For example, look how nicely Sally is crawling. She has a mental age of 8 months, and she is right on schedule. You can't imagine how long it took me to break her of that ugly old walk she had before."*

Academic Models

Severely and moderately handicapped high school students are often subjected to a second sort of norm-referenced curriculum. If it is assumed that schools are for teaching primarily academic skills, this suggests to some that handicapped students should be learning pre-academic skills and early academic skills. While there is evidence that, given careful systematic instruction, low-functioning students can learn pre-academic skills (Hofmeister & Espeseth, 1970), it seems to us that teaching pre-academic skills makes little sense if the students are likely to leave school before they go from the pre-academic to the academic level. Furthermore, many severely and moderately handicapped students are unable to apply learned academics in a useful way. When the skills are not used, they are lost, and the student has to learn to count to 50 again the next year. In other words, high school teachers teaching pre-academic and early academic skills to this population are wasting valuable time that could be spent

---

*Though seemingly laughable, this example, as well as Examples 6.2 and 6.3 that follow, actually occurred. The dialogues are presented here with minimal editorial changes.

teaching skills that would be likely to improve productivity or independence. Skills that are used immediately within a job or community setting would not have to be re-taught each year.

The common use of academics can be explained in a number of ways. First of all, teachers' commitment to academics may stem from the fact that they have often originally been trained as elementary teachers of mildly handicapped students. Teachers are simply doing what they have been trained to do. Second, parents, for whatever reasons, often view academics as being very important and lobby for the inclusion of these goals on IEPs. Finally, norm-referenced academic test scores are reassuring for teachers because such scores are familiar.

Example 6.2.

A Visit with a Student Who May Be
Inappropriately Placed in an Academic Curriculum

Consultant: "Hi, Bob, what ya working on?"
Student: "My plus fours."
Consultant: "How long have been working on them?"
Student: "Bout 6 years."
Consultant: "Six years! Isn't that a long time?"
Student: "Yup, but it's worth it."
Consultant: "How so?"
Student: "I can get an ice cream if I get 'em all right."
Consultant: "Are you going to make it? You only have a few weeks 'til summer break."
Student: "Sure, I've learned these suckers for 5 years in a row. Don't see why this year should be different."

Work Study Models

High school work study programs are designed to provide opportunities for students to become involved with in-school activities as well as with out-of-school work activities (Brolin, 1976). While in school, students might work as janitor's helpers, groundskeepers, or food service workers. When in the community, they might work in almost any kind of job. In the early seventies, one of the authors had high school work study students placed at gas stations, grocery stores, and local laundries. The major problem with that work study program was that there was often very little relationship between the skills taught in school and the skills needed on the job.

Example 6.3.

A Visit with an Ex–Work Study Teacher

Teacher: "I tried that stuff last year, and it didn't work at all!"
Consultant: "What stuff?"
Teacher: "You know, that vocational stuff."
Consultant: "What went wrong?"
Teacher: "Well, we got Sam to do a couple of jobs here at school. He swept the floor and emptied the pencil sharpeners. He was sort of a janitor's helper."

Consultant: "Did he do a bad job?"
Teacher: "Heck no! He did great! Problems happened when we got him his job downtown. He got fired in 2 days."
Consultant: "Didn't he sweep well downtown?"
Teacher: "I just told you, he could sweep just fine."
Consultant: "Why did he get fired then?"
Teacher: "Milk"
Consultant: "Milk?"
Teacher: "Yep, put the milk right on the bread every time he bagged groceries. Some people get awfully mad when you squoosh their buns!"

It has been recognized for many years that there should be a close relationship between what is needed on the job and what is done in school (Rolstoe & Frey, 1965). This suggestion is very closely related to community referencing. Furthermore, the literature suggests that work study programs were a useful approach for many students (Brice, 1966; Deno, 1960; Muller & Lewis, 1966). They were, and are, clearly a better approach than either creating a preschool for adolescents or an eternal second grade.

By 1960, work study programs were the "state-of-the-art" for handicapped high school students. When they were good, they were effective. Bad work study programs, on the other hand, were characterized by their tendency to isolate the work and the study elements of the program. In addition, in-school work stations evolved that were only tangentially related to community jobs. Therefore, students began jobs with little or no training for those jobs. In summary, when work study programs were effective in placing students in competitive employment, they tended to look a great deal like the community-referenced approach we suggest. When work study went bad, one would find a school that had not met its responsibility for instruction. It was sending untrained students to employers.

Exercises

6-1. Explain why local high schools (even in smaller communities) should consider initiating vocational programming for handicapped students.
6-2. List three inappropriate programming models commonly found in schools.

Answers to Exercises

6-1. Excellent or unusual facilities are not needed to ensure good programming; parents do not have to travel long distances to visit their children; children are not forced into adult situations at 14 years of age; and handicapped students can benefit their own communities.
6-2. Developmental, academic, and (some) work study.

MOVING TOWARD
COMMUNITY-REFERENCED VOCATIONAL PROGRAMMING

If high schools are to effectively implement PL 94-142 and address their overall mission, then they must consider appropriate outcomes for students (Brown,

Branston, Hamre-Nietupski, Pumpian, Certo, & Gruenewald, 1979; Brown, Pumpian, Baumgart, Vandeventer, Ford, Nisbet, Schroeder, & Gruenewald, 1981; Wilcox & Bellamy, 1982). Appropriate outcomes for many handicapped students could include placement in a competitive job, living and functioning independently within the community, and being successful in a postschool training program. Inappropriate outcomes would include institutionalization, placement in a more restrictive environment, and failure in a postschool vocational training program. High school curricula should be developed with the goal of increasing the number of desired outcomes and decreasing the number of undesired outcomes.

Teachers wishing to utilize community-referenced programming must identify appropriate desired outcomes for their students in their community. Several chapters in this book describe the procedures for developing a community-referenced program. These procedures are directly applicable to the development of curricula for handicapped students in high schools. Community-referenced prevocational and vocational skills, if taught in the high school, would clearly enhance the productivity and independence of handicapped students.

High schools wishing to implement community-referenced vocational training programs for handicapped students face a number of obstacles. One such obstacle is program history, which results in a lack of parental, administrative, and faculty support for change. Teachers and administrators, like many people, are often comfortable with the status quo. Even when the status quo is clearly inappropriate, it has the advantage of being predictable and appears to be easier than almost anything else. In addition, most of us have a considerable investment in the status quo. When someone suggests that there is something wrong with our program, we often take their opinion to mean that there is something wrong with us. Anyone suggesting a major shift in training emphasis at a high school will have to consider the history of the program. Many schools have a history of either providing an inappropriate curriculum or not providing one at all. Entering a local high school and suggesting that what it is doing is all wrong is not likely to be a successful approach.

Facilitating Change

A variety of approaches have been utilized to bring about change in high school special education programs. One approach (Peterson, 1982) utilized a three-step design to change the attitudes of and ultimately the programs offered by school personnel. The steps are shown in Figure 6.1.

Task Force Development   The first step in facilitating change involved the selection and training of a task force. Parents, administrators, special educators, and regular classroom teachers were selected to work on the task force. Teachers on the task force were elected by the high school faculty. Parents and administrators were invited to work on the project. Task force

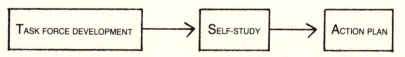

Figure 6.1. Three-step approach to changing school programs.

members met during the evening to receive training in the area of secondary special education. During these after-school sessions, task force members reviewed a variety of programming options for both mildly and more seriously handicapped students.

In addition to after-school training, task force members visited model programs in other schools, as well as adult vocational training centers. By the end of training, most task force members were aware of a variety of programming options that were available to the local district.

Self-Study The second step of the design involved the task force in a series of self-study projects. These included:

1. An investigation of the level of involvement of nonspecial education personnel in the special education process
2. An investigation of how out-of-district placements are made, including people involved, procedures, and criteria used
3. An investigation of the current functioning of handicapped students within the regular classroom and generally within the school program
4. An assessment of the level of knowledge about special education
5. A review of existing special education curriculum programming currently available to handicapped children
6. A review of existing student IEPs
7. An investigation aimed at identifying potential resources within the community
8. A complete accounting of money currently being spent on both in-school and out-of-district high school special education programs.

Once these studies were conducted, the task force had a reasonably good idea of where they were.

Action Plan The third step of the approach to facilitating change utilized a discrepancy model to develop an action plan for the district that would define where they wanted to go as well as how they were going to get there. Task force members developed a description of ideal services in each program area. They then compared what now existed with their ideal services model. Finally, the cost of a variety of ways to move from what existed to the ideal was estimated. Those estimates were presented to the school board for action.

It has been our experience that this task force approach is effective in bringing about change within a high school. Task force members become an informed group that educates other faculty members. Administrators often become advocates for handicapped students and parents become more supportive of the school.

One district that used this procedure is currently working with a nearby vocational training center to develop community-referenced programming leading to postschool employment or postschool vocational training at the adult facility. This project has broad support among faculty, administrators, and parents, and we feel it has an excellent chance for success.

One addition to the task force model might be the inclusion of adult vocational training facility staff as community members of the task force. This would serve several purposes. First of all, vocational staff would become familiar with what currently exists in their local school. Secondly, staff would, as task force members, be in a position to suggest alternatives to the three inappropriate curricular options described earlier in this chapter. Finally, several of the self-studies conducted using this model could be viewed as elements of a community-referenced approach to vocational program planning. The community resource study, for example, could be utilized to find local jobs that handicapped students could be trained to do.

Nontraditional programs need broad support if they are to survive. The procedure described above has a good chance of generating that sort of support.

Exercise

6-3. Outline a model that may be used to bring about change in a high school special education program.

Answer to Exercise

6-3. I. Task force
    A. Selection
    B. Training
    C. Visit model program
  II. Conduct self-study of:
    A. Nonspecial education involvement in the program
    B. Out-of-district placements
    C. Current functioning of handicapped students within the school
    D. Teachers' level of special education knowledge
    E. Existing programming
    F. Existing IEPs
    G. Community resources
    H. Expenditures for all special education programs
  III. Action plan
    A. Identify ideal program
    B. Develop options for going from what currently exists to the ideal
    C. Estimate the costs

Cooperative Program Implementation

Once a school district and a vocational training center have decided to implement a cooperative vocational training program, there are several potential obstacles that they may need to overcome. A few of these obstacles are:

1. Lack of school facilities and materials
2. Lack of identified local jobs
3. Lack of training procedures and curricula to teach local jobs
4. Lack of a prevocational curriculum designed for students who will graduate to an adult vocational training center
5. Shortage of teachers
6. Lack of trained teachers
7. Rules that keep teachers from leaving the school building

While it can be argued that schools could and should address these problems on their own, it clearly will not be easy. Adult community-based training programs are in a unique position to assist schools in program development. Adult programs, for example, should have already developed a working relationship with local employers. They can introduce school people to these employers and assist in the placement of high school students in competitive employment.

Curricular work done by community-referenced programs can also be shared with the school. If the auto washing task at Joe's Motors has been analyzed, and tests as well as curriculum materials have been developed by one agency, there is really no reason to reinvent the wheel (or how to wash it).

Many adult training centers have established entry criteria for their programs. School personnel may use those entry criteria to establish goals for students for whom additional postschool training seems to be required. This approach may assist school personnel in developing a prevocational curriculum based on local criteria.

Cooperative Staff Development

Many of the obstacles to effective high school program development are staff related. To overcome these obstacles a few adult vocational training programs have developed projects where high school teachers complete summer internships working with adult trainers in vocational and prevocational settings. Such internship programs serve a dual function. First of all, they provide experience and training in vocational settings, which many special education personnel lack. Second, they provide an opportunity for school and adult training facility staff to work together. This association can form a basis for cooperative program development throughout the year.

CONCLUSION

In summary, we believe that schools and adult facilities can work together to provide improved training to high school-aged handicapped students. Change at the high school level would clearly mean change at other levels of training. Some high schools are currently providing good prevocational/vocational training. We believe that they will serve as models for other schools, and eventually the relationship between the high school and adult training facilities will be affected. Staff at adult training programs can facilitate and help to direct that change by working with high schools as they develop programs for handicapped students.

SUGGESTED ACTIVITIES

1. Make a list of high school-age trainees at your facility. Discuss each of those trainees using the following questions:
   a. What high school activities could this trainee benefit from?
   b. Is there any reason why a vocation training program for this trainee could not be established in a high school?
2. Use the general guidelines set forth for this chapter to develop a specific step-by-step plan for implementing a cooperative training program with a local school system.

REFERENCES

Brice, C. R. Vocational programming for the retarded. *American Vocational Journal*, 1966, *41*(5), 23–26.

Brolin, D. E. *Vocational preparation of retarded citizens.* Columbus, OH: Charles E. Merrill Publishing Co., 1976.

Brown, L., Branston, M. B., Hamre-Nietupski, S., Pumpian, I., Certo, N., & Gruenewald, L. A strategy for developing chronological age appropriate and functional curricular content for severely handicapped adolescents and young adults. *Journal of Special Education*, 1979, *13*, 81–90.

Brown, L., Pumpian, I., Baumgart, D., Vandeventer, P., Ford, A., Nisbet, J., Schroeder, J., & Gruenewald, L. Longitudinal transition plans in programs for severely handicapped students. *Exceptional Children*, 1981, *47*, 624–630.

Deno, E. D. Vocational training for the retarded. *Exceptional Children*, 1960, *27*, 166–172.

Ferrara, J., Miller, S., Monroe, J. D., & Thompson, R. *Adjustments in instruction and curriculum for secondary special education students.* Vermillion: University of South Dakota, 1983.

Hofmeister, A., & Espeseth, V.K. Predicting academic achievement with TMR adults and teenagers. *American Journal of Mental Deficiency*, 1970, *75*, 105–107.

Lakin, K. C., Hill, B. K., Hauber, F. A., & Bruininks, R. H. Changes in age at first admission to residential care for mentally retarded people. *Mental Retardation*, 1982, *20*, 216–219.

Muller, V., & Lewis, M. A work program for the mentally retarded students. *Journal of Secondary Education*, 1966, *41*, 75–80.

Peterson, M. *Planning project for secondary special education.* Lennox, SD: Lennox School District No. 41-4, 1982.

Rolstoe, O., & Frey, R. *A high school work-study program for mentally subnormal students.* Carbondale and Edwardsville, IL: Southern Illinois University Press, 1965.

Wilcox, B., & Bellamy, G. T. *Design of high school programs for severely handicapped students.* Baltimore: Paul H. Brookes Publishing Co., 1982.

Williams, W., Brown, L., & Certo, N. Basic components of instructional programs. *Theory Into Practice*, 1975, *14*, 123–136.

VOCATIONAL EVALUATION

CHAPTER 7

Traditional
Vocational Evaluation

OBJECTIVES

To be able to:

1. List and discuss the four purposes of assessment as they relate to vocational training.

2. List and explain three proactive questions that must be addressed by vocational evaluation.

3. Define reliability, validity, and standardization.

4. List five questions related to testing issues and proactive concepts that can be used to evaluate assessment instruments.

5. Explain why the following types of tests may not facilitate vocational habilitation:
   a. Intelligence tests
   b. Academic achievement tests
   c. Motor function and manual dexterity tests
   d. Vocational aptitude tests
   e. Work samples
   f. Vocational preference tests

6. Explain how certain criterion-referenced academic achievement tests might be useful in facilitating vocational training.

7. List the advantages and disadvantages of using work samples within a community-referenced vocational training program.

One of the more difficult problems facing habilitation professionals is assessing the vocational skills of severely handicapped individuals (Revell & Wehman, 1978). While there appears to be agreement regarding the need for vocational evaluation (Brolin, 1982; Revell, Kriloff, & Sarkees, 1980; Schalock & Karan, 1979), debate continues as to the appropriate procedures, techniques, and outcomes of vocational assessment (Alper & Choisser, 1981; Mithaug, 1981; Rudrud, Ferrara, Wendelgass, Markve, & Decker, 1982; Schutz & Rusch, 1982). In order to critically evaluate the various approaches, we must first consider the purposes of assessment and review standards for designing instruments.

PURPOSES OF ASSESSMENT

Assessment can serve four purposes: diagnosis, placement, prediction, and prescription (Bernstein, Ziarnik, Rudrud, & Czajkowski, 1981).

Diagnosis

Diagnosis refers to conducting an assessment to identify the problem. For example, if we went to our family physician complaining of a fever and small spots on our skin, an assessment might lead to a diagnosis of a case of measles. The assessment procedures have resulted in a diagnosis, but the diagnosis in and of itself does not remedy our situation. Similarly, diagnoses of ''mental retardation,'' ''cerebral palsy,'' ''minimal brain dysfunction,'' or ''epilepsy'' are outcomes of assessment procedures, but the client is no better and some-times worse off once he or she is diagnosed. Oftentimes, diagnosis will lead to labeling that is detrimental to the client.

Placement

Another outcome of assessment may be placement. Placement refers to an outcome in which individuals who score similarly on an assessment battery receive special services that are designed to serve special groups. For example, in the past, persons who were severely hearing impaired were placed in a school for deaf persons. Assessment-related placements continue today. There are special programs for individuals who are diagnosed as being visually impaired, culturally disadvantaged, educable mentally retarded, trainable mentally retarded, severely/profoundly mentally retarded, autistic, brain damaged, etc. Thus, assessment can lead to placement rather than remediation.

Prediction

Assessment procedures may also result in prediction. Prediction refers to determining an outcome prior to its occurrence based upon assessment information. Prediction information is most useful to individuals who administer programs that have limited resources. A scholarship program administrator, for example, would seek to enroll only those students who are likely to succeed. An employer may seek to predict which of his employees would benefit from advanced training. Intelligence tests predict (to some degree) which students will have difficulty in regular classrooms. For example, a student with an IQ score of 70 will likely have a more difficult time in a regular classroom than a student with an IQ score of 115.

At best, prediction may identify outcomes. There are two problems associated with dependence upon predictive vocational assessment:

1. Prediction does not provide useful information for programming. In fact, the purpose of vocational training is to teach skills that will contradict predictions based on pretraining assessments.
2. Many of the instruments currently in use do not do a particularly effective job of predicting.

For instance, Timmerman and Doctor (1974) summarized studies addressing the prediction of employability of students diagnosed as trainable mentally retarded (TMR) and concluded:

> Research into the job skills of TMRs and competitive job placements being recorded by vocational rehabilitation facilities indicate that the TMR is, in many cases, capable of sheltered or competitive employment. As the present study reveals, however, the discovery of this individual potential is left almost completely to chance (p. 65).

Prescription

The most important purpose of assessment is prescription. That is, vocational evaluators should be primarily concerned with identifying, or prescribing, ways to facilitate vocational training.

Prescription Is Proactive   A proactive approach addresses the following questions:

1. Where is the trainee presently?
2. Where is the trainee going?
3. How do you get the trainee there?

Each of these questions must be addressed during vocational evaluation.

Where is the trainee presently?   The purpose of asking where the trainee is currently is to determine present level of functioning and identify relevant past experiences that may relate to habilitation programming. Examples of questions to be asked include:

1. What can the individual do?
2. What are the individual's strengths?
3. What are the individual's needs? (Bernstein et al., 1981)

Where is the trainee going? The answer to the question of where the trainee is going depends largely upon the goal of your program and your community. However, it also depends on the trainee's vocational preference.

How do you get the trainee there? Getting the trainee there is accomplished by answering questions such as:

1. What teaching techniques have been successful with the individual?
2. What teaching techniques have been unsuccessful?
3. What type and how much assistance do you have to supply? Under what conditions?
4. What resources does your agency have that can meet the individual's needs?
5. What resources are available from other agencies or within your community that can meet the individual's needs? (Bernstein et al., 1981)

Exercises

7-1. Assessment can serve four purposes. What are they?
7-2. What are three proactive questions related to prescription?

Answers to Exercises

7-1. *Diagnosis* refers to identifying the problem. *Placement* refers to using assessment information to group individuals for treatment. *Prediction* refers to determination of an outcome prior to its occurrence. *Prescription* refers to using assessment information to facilitate training.
7-2. Where is the trainee presently? Where is the trainee going? How are you going to get the trainee there?

TESTING CONCERNS

Example 7.1.

Sally was scheduled for a vocational evaluation. In the morning, one evaluator completed the assessment. In the afternoon, a second evaluator mistakenly re-administered the same tests. During the staffing, the evaluators realized that they had given the same tests and were surprised at the different scores that Sally obtained. These differences were likely due to one or more of the following: evaluator(s) did not follow standardized administration procedures, the tests themselves do not elicit the same response each time they are administered, or whatever characteristics are being measured are not stable across different testing situations. Any one of these factors can make assessment results useless.

The remainder of this chapter concerns instruments used for assessment. In addition to evaluating how well each instrument addresses the proactive questions, it is important to consider four basic testing issues: standardization, reliability, validity, and use of norms.

Standardization

Standardization refers to the procedures that are used to ensure that a test is applied and interpreted appropriately. This means first of all that the materials, directions, verbal instructions, and scoring are done in a standard manner to minimize some of the problems noted in Example 7.1.

Unfortunately, many tests require prerequisite skills (e.g., reading ability, vocabulary) that handicapped individuals may not possess. Since standardized procedures for testing must be used to obtain meaningful scores, when the person to be tested does not have the skills needed for the standardized procedure, there is no way to make a meaningful comparison between that person's score and norms obtained under standardized conditions (Salvia & Ysseldyke, 1981).

Reliability

Reliability refers to "the degree of consistency between two measures of the same thing" (Mehrens & Lehmann, 1973, p. 102). The more reliable a test is, the more consistently it measures. Some skills can be reliably measured by well-designed tests. Other skills or behaviors that are exhibited only under certain specific conditions cannot be consistently measured across other conditions. A trainee who wishes to obtain work as a janitor, for instance, may be on-task 95% of the time while doing janitorial work, but only 55% of the time while doing assembly work.

Validity

Validity refers to how well a test measures what it purports to measure (Borg & Gall, 1971). For example, suppose two tests are designed to measure janitorial skills. One test is comprised of test items directly taken from jobs janitors do; the other test requires the individual to sort objects by shape, size, and color. The first test is said to be valid because the test items are direct measures of skills needed by a janitor. The second test may not have validity since sorting by shape, size, and color are not typical janitorial skills.

Another way of looking at validity involves considering how well a test predicts future outcomes. For example, if a test is designed to predict competitive job placement, you would give the test to a group of individuals and when that group was competitively employed you would compare their individual test scores with the outcome (competitive employment) and see if the scores predicted success in competitive employment.

Use of Norms

The populations on which most traditional vocational assessments are normed do not include a broad range of handicapped individuals. Thus, the validity of these instruments is often questioned (Alper & Choisser, 1981; Botterbusch,

1976, 1977, 1980; Brolin, 1976; Gold, 1973). Perhaps more important, however, is the question of how norms will be used. Suppose the norms show average scores on an instrument for competitively employed persons who hold jobs similar to a trainee's intended occupation. These norms can be used to determine how closely trainee performance resembles that of successful workers, and what remains to be learned. Comparison of an individual's score to norms based on a group of handicapped individuals is therefore unlikely to be useful unless the handicapped persons in the norm group are also successfully employed. Norm groups should be evaluated based on their intended use, not merely on whether they contain persons with handicapping conditions.

In summary, before adopting any test or testing system, vocational training facilities should ask the following questions:

1. Does this test help us to know how the trainee stands in terms of vocational skills?
2. Does this test help us to determine where he or she is going?
3. Does this test help us to determine how to teach the individual?
4. Do the test items measure the skills needed for competitive employment opportunities within my community?
5. Has the test been shown to be a reliable measure of trainee skills?

Exercises

7-3. Give an example of problems in the areas of validity, reliability, and standardization.
7-4. What questions should you ask regarding assessment instruments?

Answers to Exercises

7-3. *Validity Problems* are the result of tests that do not measure what they purport to measure. An example would be a vocational achievement test that measures language ability, not vocational achievement. *Reliability Problems* are the result of tests that do not measure consistently. A test that results in radically different scores for the same individual when administered by two competent examiners would be an example of a test with reliability problems. *Standardization Problems* are the result of tests that are not consistently applied or interpreted. For example, evaluators use different verbal instructions with different clients, or interpret scores for adults using standards developed for children.
7-4. Does the test address the three proactive questions: Where are you presently? Where are you going? How will you get there? Does the test satisfy accepted standards for validity, reliability, and standardization?

COMMONLY USED STANDARDIZED VOCATIONAL ASSESSMENT INSTRUMENTS

The following sections discuss the more common instruments and approaches that are used in the vocational evaluation process. (Publishers of all tests reviewed are listed in the Appendix to this chapter.) Readers are encouraged to stay abreast of changes in the vocational evaluation field by reading journals such as *The Vocational Evaluation and Work Adjustment Bulletin*, which is published by the Vocational Evaluation and Work Adjustment Association of the National Rehabilitation Association. Remember to ask the five questions listed above about each instrument you consider using for vocational evaluations.

Intelligence Tests

Intelligence tests are designed to assess how an individual scores relative to the general population on a variety of verbal and cognitive performance tasks. There is considerable controversy regarding their use in general, but surprisingly little controversy regarding their use in vocational planning and assessment. Brolin (1976, 1982) noted what he termed the "perplexing phenomenon" of the importance attached to an IQ score for vocational planning. Intelligence tests do not provide information to vocational trainers that is useful in either prediction or program planning. Further, the IQ has little if any relevance when individualized programs are used (Striefel & Cadez, 1983).

Educational Achievement Tests

The educational assessment serves to identify and evaluate an individual's academic abilities. There are two types of commercially available tests that could be used by vocational training facilities: norm-referenced and criterion-referenced tests. Norm-referenced tests are referenced to a sample assumed to be representative of a larger population (Salvia & Ysseldyke, 1981). Most have not included adult handicapped persons in their standardization populations. The best that trainers can expect to get from these instruments is a rough idea about the trainees' academic achievement.

The second type of test that is available is the criterion-referenced test. These instruments "measure a person's development of particular skills in terms of absolute levels of mastery" (Salvia & Ysseldyke, 1981, p. 30). Typically, these instruments provide evaluators with a wide variety of test items covering specific behavioral responses. The evaluator must choose test items that measure skills that are of potential value to the trainee. It is possible, therefore, to use individual items from these tests to construct an instrument that assesses the training needs of clients. People using this strategy should keep in mind that the majority of the skills tested are taught in academic settings and may not be appropriate to vocational situations. We believe, however, that elements of criterion-referenced tests may have potential utility for some vocational trainees.

Norm-Referenced Achievement Tests

Wide Range Achievement Test (WRAT) The WRAT can be administered quickly and provides measures of reading (word attack and recognition), spelling, and mathematics. The testing range is from kindergarten through college.

Peabody Individual Achievement Test (PIAT) The PIAT provides assessment of mathematics, reading recognition, reading comprehension, spelling, and general information. Test items are presented orally and the respondent indicates the correct answer among four alternatives, illustrations, numbers, words, or sentences. Test items cover kindergarten through grade 12.

Adult Basic Learning Examination (ABLE) The ABLE was designed to assess educational achievement of adults with little or no formal education. The ABLE measures vocabulary, reading, spelling, and arithmetic. There are three levels of the test: Level 1 is for grades 1–4; Level 2 for grades 5–8; and Level 3 is for grades 9–12.

Criterion-Referenced Achievement Tests

SCAT Skill Screener The SCAT Skill Screener is a criterion-referenced test that evaluates ability in the area of beginning reading as well as beginning mathematics. Items test abilities in math ranging from copying numbers through fractions and decimals. Reading skills range from matching and copying numbers through reading 100-word passages.

Key Math Diagnostic Arithmetic Test The Key Math is a diagnostic skill screener that is designed to be criterion-referenced in three general mathematics areas: content, operation, and application. One strength of this test is that it provides specific information about performance that can be used to develop instructional goals. In addition, the test has been normed on kindergarten through seventh grade children and grade equivalent norm-referenced scores can be calculated.

Brigance Diagnostic Inventory of Basic Skills There are three Brigance Skill Inventories available. *The Inventory of Early Development* and *Inventory of Basic Skills* are designed to test skills that are typically learned by children from birth through sixth grade. *The Inventory of Essential Skills* provides items covering skills in reading, language arts, and math that are typically learned from grades 2 through 10. In addition, items are provided in the areas of health and safety, vocational training, money and finance, travel and transportation, food and clothing, as well as communication skills. All three inventories provide items that are clearly related to behavioral objectives.

Exercise

7-5. How can criterion-referenced academic achievement tests be useful to vocational trainers?

Answer to Exercise

7-5. Specific test items may address objectives needed by the individual. Examiners can select and administer those items that are directly related to skills needed by the trainee.

Vocational Aptitude Tests

There is some question whether there is a real distinction between aptitude and achievement tests. Aptitude test proponents argue that aptitude tests serve to predict subsequent performance and are used to estimate the extent to which the individual will profit from a particular type of training (Anastasi, 1982). The achievement tests described above measure current academic performance. The use of aptitude tests with severely handicapped individuals has been questioned because: a) the tests were not intended for this population; b) the tests require fairly sophisticated reading, mathematical, and vocabulary skills; and c) severely handicapped individuals were not included in the norm groups.

General Aptitude Test Battery (GATB) The GATB was designed to assess vocational aptitudes for use in vocational counseling, job selection, and job placement. Nine aptitudes are measured (general learning ability, verbal aptitude, numerical ability, spatial aptitude, form perception, clerical perception, motor coordination, finger dexterity, and manual dexterity) that are related to approximately 500 occupations, primarily of the unskilled or semi-skilled type. The subtests include eight paper-and-pencil items and four performance items. Disadvantages of the GATB are: all tests are highly speeded, coverage of aptitudes is somewhat limited, and a sixth-grade reading knowledge is recommended (Anastasi, 1982). Also, the validity of the GATB has been questioned.

Non-Reading Aptitude Test Battery (NATB) The NATB was developed to compensate for the limitations of the GATB for disadvantaged individuals and those with less academic background. The battery was designed to measure the same nine aptitude scores as the GATB and consists of two subtests, but requires no reading or writing. Anastasi (1982) reported that the results of the nonreading battery have proved to be disappointing, that it has not been widely adopted, and that the NATB will likely be discontinued.

Differential Aptitude Tests (DAT) The DAT was designed for use in the educational and vocational counseling of students in grades 8–12. The DAT provides measures of verbal reasoning, numerical ability, abstract reasoning, clerical speed and accuracy, mechanical reasoning, space relations, spelling, and language usage. The DAT calls for a sixth-grade reading level and is normed on grades 8–12.

Motor Functioning and Manual Dexterity Tests

The major problem with motor functioning and manual dexterity tests is that they measure skills that may not be related to specific vocational behaviors. For example, the Bender Visual Motor Gestalt Test requires the examinee to draw a geometric figure that is presented on a card. Except for a few fields such as drafting, architecture, and art, drawing geometric figures is a seldom-used task. It has been the authors' experience that few severely handicapped individuals have been able to correctly draw these figures, yet this inability has not hindered their vocational training.

These tests attempt to measure general ability in the areas of fine motor functioning and manual dexterity, as well as speed and eye-hand coordination. In addition, some of these tests have been interpreted as indicators of deviant psychological functioning (i.e., neurological impairment and emotional disturbance).

While this general information may be nice to know, what trainers really need are precise data describing how well a trainee can do each specific part of a job. Fine motor coordination as measured by these tests may or may not be related to a specific job. For example, while fine motor coordination may be related to the assembly of electronic circuit boards, a more valid and reliable measure of the ability to assemble circuit boards would involve the use of a circuit board assembly.

Bennett Hand Tool Dexterity Test　The Bennett Hand Tool Dexterity Test provides a measure of proficiency in using ordinary mechanic tools. It consists of 9 or 12 nuts, bolts, and washers of three different sizes on a hard wood frame. The trainee must transfer the bolts, washers, and nuts to the other side as quickly as possible using two wrenches and a screwdriver. The scoring is done by clocking the total time required for the completion of the task. Brolin (1976) indicated that a major problem in utilizing this test with retarded individuals is the difficulty they have in understanding, remembering, and following the directions.

Purdue Pegboard　The Purdue Pegboard test measures gross movements of hands, fingers, and arms, and finger-tip dexterity. The pegboard has two rows of 25 holes and four cups containing pins, washers, and collars. During administration, pins are inserted individually in the holes with the right hand, left hand, and both hands together. The fourth administration involves assembling, within 1 minute, the pins, washers, and collars using both hands. Results are compared with norms for industrial workers and college students.

Crawford Small Parts Dexterity Test　Designed to measure fine eye-hand coordination, the Crawford Small Parts Dexterity Test consists of a board containing 42 holes on the left and right bottom portions with three bins for pins, collars, and screws across the top. In Part I of the test, the trainee uses tweezers to pick up a pin and insert it into close-fitting holes, and then places a small collar over each pin. In Part II, small screws are placed in threaded holes and screwed down with a screwdriver. Scoring is based on the time reqired to complete each part. The norm groups for this test are factory workers (Brolin, 1976).

O'Connor Finger Dexterity and O'Connor Tweezer Dexterity Tests　The O'Connor Finger Dexterity and Tweezer Dexterity Tests are designed to assess motor coordination and finger and manual dexterity. Both tests use plates with 100 holes arranged in 10 rows. The finger dexterity test requires the insertion, as rapidly as possible, of three small metal pins into each of the holes. The tweezer dexterity test involves using a metal tweezer to pick up the pins, one by one from the tray, and insert them into each of the 100 holes. Scoring is based on the time it takes to complete each test.

Stromberg Dexterity Test The Stromberg Dexterity Test is designed to measure speed and accuracy of arm and hand movement. The test requires the client to insert 54 red, blue, and yellow disks in corresponding colored holes of a board. The client is allowed two practice trials and then is scored on the amount of time required to complete the task on the third and fourth trials. Brolin (1976) reported that the test has seven norm groups, but little information is available about them.

Bender Visual Motor Gestalt Test The Bender Visual Motor Gestalt Test (Bender Gestalt) is a perceptual-motor test that may be useful in indicating brain damage and assessing visual perception. The test has also been used to assess emotional disturbance. It consists of nine designs, each on individual cards. The examinee is asked to copy the designs. Several authors have questioned the reliability and validity of the Bender Gestalt (Brolin, 1976; Salvia & Ysseldyke, 1981).

Vocational Interest Inventories

Vocational interest inventories were designed to assess an individual's interests in different fields of work. The use of interest inventories with severely handicapped individuals is questionable for several reasons:

1. The more commonly used interest inventories require high verbal, vocabulary, and reading abilities.
2. Common interest inventories ask an individual to choose between several experiences and/or jobs. Handicapped individuals may have limited exposure or knowledge of some or all of these experiences and/or jobs.
3. Interest inventories may not reflect jobs available in the community. Many interest inventories are based on very traditional, stereotypic assumptions concerning jobs that are suitable for men and jobs that are suitable for women. These assumptions may not reflect current social assumptions. We are opposed to preventing expression of interest in an occupation based solely upon whether an individual is male or female.

Strong-Campbell Interest Inventory The Strong-Campbell Interest Inventory is comprised of 325 items grouped into seven parts. The inventory provides scores for six general occupational themes, 23 basic interest scales, and 124 occupational scales. The scores serve as an index of similarity between a person's interests and the interests of successful individuals in a variety of occupations. Bitter (1979) indicated that this inventory has been most useful for identifying vocational goals that require a college education.

Kuder Occupational Interest Survey Survey items contain three short statements of different activities and the individual must choose the most preferred and least preferred activities. The individual's score on each occupational scale is expressed as a correlation between his or her interest pattern and the interest pattern of a particular occupational group. Scores are available for 127 specific occupational groups and 48 college majors. This inventory requires a better than seventh grade reading ability (Bitter, 1979).

Geist Picture Interest Inventory (GPII) The Geist Picture Interest Inventory is designed to assess interests in 11 areas. There are 44 items on the test, each item consisisting of three drawings of various job activities (e.g., worker pruning a tree) and related materials (such as tools of the trade) with captions under each item asking such questions as, "Which would you rather do for a living?" Norms are provided for grades 8–12, for trade schools, and universities.

Vocational Interest and Sophistication Assessment (VISA) The Vocational Interest and Sophistication Assessment instrument was designed to assess vocational interests of educable mentally retarded students. The VISA is a reading-free test consisting of line drawings of people (75 pictures of male forms and 53 pictures of female forms) working at various jobs. The trainee is shown each drawing and asked if he or she would like to perform the work shown "a lot," "a little," or "not at all." The male form provides interest scores in seven areas: garage, laundry, food service, maintenance, farm and town, materials handling, and industry. The female form provides scores in four areas: business and clerical, food service, housekeeping, and laundry. The sophistication portion of the VISA consists of a series of questions designed to assess the trainee's knowledge of the illustrated job areas.

Wide Range Interest-Opinion Test (WRIOT) The WRIOT is another nonreading picture interest test that is comprised of 150 sets of three pictures. The individual is asked to identify which picture he or she likes most and likes least in each set. The results are given in 18 job clusters and interest areas including: art, drama, sales, management, social service, number, mechanics, and outdoor. Norms are provided for the general population of 10th and 11th grade high school students.

AAMD-Becker Reading-Free Vocational Interest Inventory (RFVII) The RFVII was designed to assess vocational preferences among mentally retarded individuals. There are male and female forms of the test. The male form provides measures of preference among 11 job clusters: automotive, building trades, clerical, animal care, food service, patient care, horticulture, janitorial, personal service, laundry service, and materials handling. The female form assesses preferences from eight job clusters: laundry, light industrial, clerical, personal service, food service, patient care, horticulture, and housekeeping. The person is presented with a set of three line drawings depicting various vocational activities, and must select the most preferred activity. Preference for each area is determined by the number of times an item is selected from a job cluster. Male and female norms are provided for public day school, institutionalized, and composite groups of mentally retarded persons.

Reading-Free Vocational Interest Inventory   The Reading-Free Vocational Interest Inventory is the revised version of the AAMD-Becker. This version was normed on learning disabled and mentally retarded individuals. In addition, the test does not have a male and female form, rather a single form consisting of 165 illustrations arranged in groups of three's, assessing 11 interest clusters. Norms are provided for public school, educable mentally retarded, learning disabled, and adult sheltered workshop populations.

Work Samples

Work samples were devised as an alternative method of vocational assessment in response to the criticisms of traditional vocational evaluation. *Simulated job samples* provide a representation of the common critical factors of a job. They are, by definition, more limited than actual job samples because it is difficult to simulate variables such as working outdoors under different weather conditions or numbers of other employees or customers present. *Single trait samples* assess a single worker trait or characteristic. The trait may have relevance to a specific job or many jobs. *Cluster trait samples* assess a number of traits in a job or variety of jobs. The cluster trait sample is based upon an analysis of an occupational grouping and identification of traits presumed necessary for successful performance.

The advantages of work samples in vocational evaluation are listed below.

1. Work samples may be more flexible than psychometric tests in that their administration can be varied to meet the individual needs of clients (Pruitt, 1977).
2. Work samples may reflect the real world of work by assessing the same skills, aptitudes, and abilities required in competitive employment situations (Brolin, 1976; Mithaug, 1981; Schalock & Karan, 1979).
3. Work samples provide the opportunity to directly observe actual work behavior in a controlled setting (Brolin, 1976).
4. Work samples can provide exposure to and experience in a wide range of jobs.
5. Performance on work samples may be less affected than performance on psychometric tests by sensorimotor impairments, educational deficiencies, or language disabilities (Schalock & Karan, 1979).
6. Prospective employers will generally welcome reports of work sample performance more than test scores (Brolin, 1976).

Potential disadvantages of work samples are listed below.

1. Work samples may not reflect actual job availability within the community (Bitter, 1979; Rudrud et al., 1982)
2. Many work samples do not have satisfactory levels of reliability and have not been sufficiently validated (Botterbusch, 1976, 1977, 1980).

3. The resemblance of work samples to actual jobs does not ensure their predictive validity due to the inability to duplicate the entire job via work samples, the sometimes subjective nature of the evaluation format, and/or the lack of standardization among work samples (Brolin, 1976).

4. Commercially available work samples are usually quite expensive, local samples take a long time to develop, and both will need periodic revisions so that they do not become obsolete (Pruitt, 1977).

5. Several commercial work samples require prerequisite reading skills that many handicapped individuals do not have (Botterbusch, 1976, 1980, Stodden, Casale, & Schwartz, 1977).

TOWER System   The TOWER System (Testing, Orientation, and Work Evaluation in Rehabilitation) was designed for physically and emotionally disabled individuals. Industrial norms are not available (Botterbusch, 1976; Pruitt, 1977). The TOWER provides 110 work samples in the following 14 areas: clerical, drafting, drawing, electronics assembly, jewelry manufacturing, leather goods, machine shop, machine lettering, mail clerk, optical mechanics, pantograph engraving, sewing machine operating, welding, and workshop assembly. Pruitt (1977) notes that a number of these areas reflect jobs that are unique to the New York City area and may not relate to jobs within other communities. The work samples progress in difficulty from simple to complex within each area. Trainees are given the opportunity to practice using the tools of a particular occupational area prior to evaluation, and occupational areas to be assessed are then selected by the evaluator, who considers the individual's stated interests as well as his or her level of functioning, assets, and limitations (Bitter, 1979). Performance is rated according to time, error, and quality standards based on five-point scales ranging from superior to inferior. A thorough evaluation utilizing the TOWER system requires about 3 weeks and evaluators must participate in a 3-week training program to be certified in the use of the TOWER.

Pruitt (1977) reported that no reliability data were available for the TOWER. Not surprisingly, the validity of the TOWER has also been seriously questioned (Pruitt, 1977; Timmerman & Doctor, 1974).

> The TOWER System is the oldest complete work evaluation system and over the years has served as a model for the development of many work samples . . . . The lack of precise definitions for work performance factors and client behaviors and the lack of adequate norms are the major weaknesses of the system. The high use of written instructions and the high level of the areas evaluated restricts its use with low literate and mentally retarded clients (Botterbusch, 1980, p. 76).

Philadelphia Jewish Employment and Vocational Service Work Sample System (JEVS)   The JEVS was originally designed for disadvantaged persons, and a modified version (Vocational Information and Evaluation Work Samples, VIEWS) has been developed for use with developmentally disabled individuals (Bitter, 1979; Brolin, 1976). The JEVS consists of 28 work samples that relate to 10 worker trait groups: handling; sorting, inspecting, measuring, and related work; tending; manipulating; routine checking and recording; classifying, filing, and related work; inspecting and stock checking; craftsmanship and related work; costuming, tailoring, and dressmaking; drafting and related work.

The work samples, ranging from simple to complex, are individually administered. The time to complete the evaluation is estimated from 6 to 7 days (Botterbusch, 1980) to 2 weeks (Bitter, 1979). During administration, work personality characteristics are observed. This includes: reaction to supervision, ability to follow directions, learning characteristics, interpersonal relationships, persistence, dependability, frustration tolerance, reaction to praise and criticism, language, attention span, independence, initiative, motivation, social skills, punctuality, attendance, and grooming. Scoring takes into account the time necessary for completion, errors, and quality of responses.

The JEVS was normed on a total population of over 1,100 clients in 32 facilities throughout the United States. However, no means, standard deviations, or percentile cutoffs are given (Botterbusch, 1980). Pruitt (1977) indicated that reliability of the work samples has not been reported and that validity data were inconclusive. Further, Stodden et al. (1977) reported that the JEVS was not appropriate for use with mentally retarded individuals for a variety of reasons, including the reading levels required.

> The strongest points of the system are its stress upon careful observation and accurate recording of work behaviors and performance factors . . . . The major problems with the system appear to be the abstract nature of many of the work samples, which hinders vocational exploration; limited evaluation feedback to the client; and the lack of job information presented to the client (Botterbusch, 1980, p. 55).

Vocational Information and Evaluation Work Samples (VIEWS) The VIEWS is a modification of the JEVS, and was designed to evaluate mildly, moderately, and severely mentally retarded individuals. The VIEWS contains 16 work samples from four categories that relate to six worker traits. The four categories are:

1. Elemental—title sorting; nuts, bolts, and washers sorting; paper counting and paper cutting; collating and stapling; stamping; nuts, bolts, and washers assembly; screen assembly; and machine feeding
2. Clerical—mail sorting; mail counting; nut weighing; and valve disassembly
3. Machine—drill press
4. Crafts—budgette assembly; valve assembly; and circuit board assembly

An important difference between the JEVS and the VIEWS is that the VIEWS distinguishes between acquisition and performance. Formal evaluation does not occur until a predetermined level of competence is reached.

Scoring is based on a three-point rating scale that reflects time and quality standards. It is estimated that between 20 and 35 hours are necessary to complete the battery. The VIEWS was normed on 104 mentally retarded individuals (median IQ = 50) with an age range from 16 to 61. No reliability or validity data are available (Botterbusch, 1977), thus making the usefulness of the VIEWS questionable at best.

McCarron-Dial Work Evaluation System (MDS)   The McCarron-Dial contains 17 instruments grouped into the following areas:

Verbal cognitive ability—Wechsler Adult Intelligence Scale–Revised (WAIS) or Stanford-Binet Intelligence Scale and Peabody Picture Vocabulary Test
Sensory—Bender Visual Motor Gestalt Test (BVMGT) and Haptic Visual Discrimination Test (HVDT)
Motor Skills—McCarron Assessment of Neuromuscular Development (MAND)
Emotional—Observational Emotional Inventory
Integration and coping—San Francisco Vocational Competency Scale and Dial Behavioral Rating Scale.

The MDS was developed to assess ability to function in day care, work activities, extended employment, transitional employment, or community employment. The MDS can be completed within a 2-week period and an evaluator must receive training in administering and interpreting the battery.

The MDS is a reasonably good predictor of vocational outcome (Dial & Swearingen, 1976; Fortune & Eldredge, 1982) in the absence of effective vocational habilitation services. In the presence of effective training, for instance at Goodwill–Denver, clients consistently achieve far greater success than predicted by the MDS, which is required by some referral sources.

Valpar Component Work Sample Series (VALPAR)   The Valpar Component Work Sample Series was designed for industrially injured workers. The VALPAR consists of 16 work samples including: small tools (mechanical), size discrimination, clerical comprehension and aptitude, numerical sorting, upper extremity range of motion, independent problem-solving, multilevel sorting, simulated assembly, whole body range of motion, tri-level measurement, eye-hand-foot coordination, soldering and inspection (electronic), money handling, integrated peer performance, electrical circuitry and print reading, and drafting. The work samples were designed to be used as individual components. The manual for each work sample identifies specific occupations and related classifications in a variety of job families related to the work sample.

Individuals being tested are provided with both verbal instructions and demonstrations. Practice trials are given to ensure that the client understands the task before the work sample is timed. Reading is not required except when necessary to perform the task. The total performance score combines time and error scores. The VALPAR work samples were normed on mentally retarded individuals, Air Force enlisted personnel, employed workers, deaf persons, skill center trainees, and community college students. Time, error, and performance scores are provided for each group.

Two major problems with the VALPAR are listed below.

1. Because the individual work samples can be purchased separately, there are no unified final report forms and the VALPAR is not an integrated system.
2. Relationships between the work samples and jobs or worker traits is unclear (Botterbusch, 1980).

Pre-Vocational Readiness Battery (VALPAR 17) The Pre-Vocational Readiness Battery (developed and marketed by the VALPAR Corporation) was designed to assess functional skills of mentally retarded individuals. The battery contains five areas, each of which has several subtests.

1. *Developmental Assessment* contains four measures of physical and mental abilities: a) patterning, color discriminations, and manipulation of colored pins in sorting trays and pattern boards; b) manual coordination that uses a stylus and maze to assess head steadiness and eye-hand coordination; c) work range, dynamic strength, and walking consisting of two charts, balance blocks, weights and lifting apparatus; and d) a series of pictorial tasks such as matching, vocational knowledge, and measurement that allow the clients to estimate length, size, and volume (other activities assess familiarity with basic tools and their functions).
2. *Workshop Evaluation* consists of a simulated assembly process in which three trainees work together on a three-step assembly task.
3. *Vocational Interest Screening* is a slide/tape presentation (90 slides) depicting jobs and providing descriptions for the client. The client compares two jobs and scores are provided for six job areas: social service, sales, machine operation, office work/clerical, physical sciences, and outdoor.
4. *Social/Interpersonal Skills* is a rating instrument containing descriptions of behaviors including personal skills, socialization skills, aggravating behaviors, and work-related skills.
5. *Independent Living Skills* evaluates four areas: transportation, money handling, grooming, and living environments.

The VALPAR 17 is intended to assess an individual's interests, vocational skills, and social maturity. However, the major problems are in the technical areas.

The manuals contain no background as to why certain components were selected, no relationship to previous work done in this field. No data are given on reliability and validity; there is not even a statement on these two factors. The norms data are impossible to interpret without additional information (p. 62).

Wide Range Employment Sample Test (WREST)   The WREST consists of 10 work samples and was designed to evaluate dexterity and perceptual abilities. The 10 work samples include: folding (single and double folding, gluing, labeling, and envelope stuffing); stapling (stapling accuracy and collation/stapling); packaging; measuring; stringing; gluing; collating; color matching; pattern matching; and assembling. Instructions are given verbally and by demonstration. The test taker has the opportunity to practice the exercises prior to timing the work sample. Scoring is based on the time required to complete the work sample. Time and quality norms are available on the general population, sheltered workshop employees, and competitively employed workers.

> Although it is not stated in the manual, the WREST seems most useful in assessing new clients for assignment to suitable work projects within a sheltered workshop . . . . The major problems of the system center around the lack of systematic behavior observations, failure to relate results to the competitive job market, and the apparent lack of a usable final report for the referring counselor or agency (Botterbusch, 1980, p. 106).

Exercises

7-6.   List the advantages of work samples.
7-7.   List the disadvantages of work samples.

Answers to Exercises

7-6.   a.   Work samples may be more flexible than psychometric tests.
　　　b.   Work samples may reflect the real world of work.
　　　c.   Work samples provide the opportunity to directly observe actual work behavior.
　　　d.   Work samples can provide exposure to and experience in a wide range of jobs.
　　　e.   Performance on work samples may be less affected by sensorimotor impairments, educational deficiencies, and language disabilities than psychometric tests.
　　　f.   Prospective employers generally welcome reports of work sample performance more than test scores.
7-7.   a.   Work samples may not reflect actual job availability within the community.
　　　b.   Many work samples do not have satisfactory levels of reliability and/or validity.
　　　c.   Work samples may not duplicate the entire job.
　　　d.   Work samples are expensive and need periodic revisions.
　　　e.   Work samples may require prerequisite skills such as reading, tool usage, etc. that many handicapped individuals do not have.

Client Rating Instruments

Client rating scales are widely used in applied rehabilitation settings and this is due to the utility of these instruments (e.g., ease of adminstration and minimum expenditure of staff time and energy). Esser (1975) stated that while client rating scales are not a panacea, when rating scales are adequately developed, they may serve a number of functions including:

1. Identifying and pinpointing positive and negative work behaviors
2. Providing information that serves as a basis for formulating goals for work adjustment or behavior change programs
3. Determining a client's status within a program at any given point in time
4. Measuring a program's effectiveness in bringing about the acquisition of positive skills and behaviors
5. Sharing information and facilitating communication

Unfortunately, few of the client rating scales presently available were adequately developed. One major problem is that rating involves subjective judgments and thus reliability among observers is often not obtained. In other words, two different staff members may rate the individual differently. Others are often normed entirely on handicapped persons. Remember, we are training for competitive employment, not comparing individuals with handicapped populations. And, last, many client rating scales are based on the assessment of excessive, maladaptive behaviors that still leave unanswered the question, "What do we want the individual to do?"

AAMD Adaptive Behavior Scales There are two versions of the Adaptive Behavior Scales: the 1974 revision of the AAMD Adaptive Behavior Scale, and the public school version. The Scale was designed to measure adaptive behavior, which is defined as "the effectiveness of an individual in coping with the natural and social demands of his or her environment." The Adaptive Behavior Scale is divided into two parts; part one measures independence in daily living, and part two measures maladaptive/inappropriate behaviors. Each item on the scale provides a numerical score that is then tallied within a subdomain or domain score. The domain scores are then converted to percentile ranks based upon age group norms. The first edition was normed on approximately 4,000 mentally retarded institutionalized individuals and the public school version was normed on 2,600 mentally retarded school children in California.

Salvia and Yesseldyke (1981) note that there are numerous problems with the Adaptive Behavior Scale. Interrater reliability is extremely low, items are overly value laden, and the scale lacks proportion (e.g., rape is weighted the same as being overly seductive in appearance). This leads Salvia & Yesseldyke (1981) to conclude that, "at its present stage of development the scale does not appear adequate for making important educational decisions about individuals'' (p. 441).

MDC Behavior Identification Format–1974 The MDC Behavior Identification Format was developed as a tool to be used in observing, identifying, and recording work and work-related behaviors that may limit or enhance employment opportunities for vocational rehabilitation clients (Esser, 1975). The Behavior Identification Format consists of 22 behavior categories such as hygiene, grooming and dress, odd or inappropriate behaviors, communication skills as related to work needs, attendance, ability to cope with work problems (frustration tolerance), stamina, steadiness or consistency of work, social skills in relations with co-workers, and work method and organization of tools and materials.

Behaviors within the categories are then rated by an observer as being A (acceptable), B (selective placement in a job where these behaviors will not interfere substantially with work performance), or C (change needed for successful employment). The Behavior Identification Form does not yield a score for comparison but is intended to describe specific client behavior and monitor progress on problem behaviors.

San Francisco Vocational Competency Scale The San Francisco Vocational Competency Scale consists of 30 items relating to four areas of vocational competence: motor skills, cognition, responsibility, and social-emotional behavior. Each item is rated according to one of four or five statements or terms that apply to the item. For example, if a client is to be rated on transferring previously learned skills to a new task, the evaluator rates the client on a scale from 1 to 5, with 1 being "hardly ever" and 5 being "nearly always." The total score can be used as a percentile score to reflect the client's standing relative to the norm group. The norm group was composed of 562 mentally retarded male and female workshop clients from 45 workshops from all regions of the country.

Work Adjustment Rating Form (WARF) The Work Adjustment Rating Form was designed to provide a measure of job readiness as it related to mentally retarded workshop clients. The Work Adjustment Rating Form contains 40 items divided into eight subscales of work behaviors. The subscales include: amount of supervision required, realism of job goals, team work, acceptance of rules/authority, work tolerance, perseverance in work, extent trainee seeks assistance, and importance attached to job training. A profile of the client's strengths and limitations can be obtained by inspection of WARF subscale scores (Bitter, 1979).

Prevocational Assessment and Curriculum Guide (PACG) The PACG was designed to assess support behaviors that a student needs for job entry and to perform well on any job (Mithaug, 1981). The behaviors identified were assessed by surveying sheltered workshops in five northwestern states and Kansas, and by asking supervisors to indicate worker behaviors that they considered important for entry into sheltered employment (Johnson & Mithaug, 1978; Mithaug & Hagmeier, 1978). Behaviors that were considered important by 85% or more of the respondents were included in the PACG. The PACG contains 46 items that assess the client's vocational skills and related work behaviors. These items are clustered into nine categories that include: attendance/endurance, independence, production, learning, behavior, communication skills, social skills, grooming and eating skills, and toileting skills. Scores for each category are plotted on a profile sheet that shows the relation between current skill level and the requirement for entry into sheltered employment. The PACG also contains a curriculum guide that lists the training goals for each assessment item in the inventory.

Sioux Vocational School Social-Interpersonal Behavior Checklist The Sioux Vocational School Social-Interpersonal Behavior Checklist was designed to be used as a screening tool that would identify individual programming needs in the social-interpersonal skills area (Bernstein, Van Soest, & Hansum, 1982). The authors caution that the checklist was not intended for use as a precise measure of individual client behavior change but rather intended to assist program planners in identifying client needs in the area of social-interpersonal behavior. The checklist contains 23 social-interpersonal behaviors, each of which is rated as being a definite need, minimally acceptable, or definite strength (see Chapter 10 for a copy of the checklist).

CONCLUSIONS

At one time or another, most of us have been exposed to some of the instruments described in this chapter. For example, the Kuder Occupational Interest Survey is often administered to high school students to assist in vocational planning. Two of the authors completed the test and found that forestry was their preferred occupation. While the other authors may regret the failure of these two to follow this recommendation, their career decisions demonstrate a critical difference between the way handicapped and nonhandicapped people are treated. The two authors could easily ignore the results of the preference inventory; handicapped individuals often cannot. Their lives may be profoundly affected by test results.

Twenty years ago, being diagnosed as mentally retarded most likely meant that you would be placed in an institution, excluded from society. When a vocational test states the client is functioning in the "activity center range" and production is "inconsequential," the individual is often excluded from opportunities for competitive employment.

Unlike most people, handicapped persons often do precisely what the vocational evaluation says they should do. This is not to say that this is always bad or that evaluators do not have their clients' best interests at heart. We simply believe that since vocational evaluators' recommendations for handicapped persons are likely to have a direct impact upon trainees' lives, we must be very careful about the assessment procedures used. When decisions are made, they should be based upon information that is appropriate and accurate. We must always remember: ''for severely handicapped persons entering the rehabilitation system who do not have satisfactory skill levels at the time of their assessment, the predictive model of vocational assessment is discriminatory at best and all too often exclusionary'' (Schalock & Karan, 1979, p. 36).

Exercise

7-8. How does the concept of exclusion relate to vocational evaluation?

Answer to Exercise

7-8. Vocational evaluation data are often used to make decisions that exclude handicapped individuals from training options.

SUGGESTED ACTIVITIES

1. Take one assessment instrument used by your facility and determine if the items on the instrument are clearly and obviously related to any of the training programs available in your facility.
2. Examine evaluators' reports, and place test scores in three categories: a) directly useful to trainers, b) somewhat useful to trainers, and c) not useful to trainers.
3. Repeat the process described in number 2 above for administrator rather than trainer concerns.
4. Look up the reliability, validity, and standardization data regarding the vocational evaluation instruments used by your facility.
5. Determine whether the evaluation instruments used by your facility answer the proactive questions discussed at the beginning of this chapter.

REFERENCES

Alper, S., & Choisser, L. Community-referenced vocational assessment of the severely handicapped. *Vocational Evaluation and Work Adjustment Bulletin*, 1981, *14*, 70–73.

Anastasi, A. *Psychological testing* (5th ed.). New York: Macmillan Publishing Co., 1982.

Bernstein, G. S., Van Soest, F., & Hansum, D. A social-interpersonal behavior screening instrument for rehabilitation facilities. *Vocational Evaluation and Work Adjustment Bulletin*, 1982, *15*, 107–111.

Bernstein, G. S., Ziarnik, J. P., Rudrud, E. H., & Czajkowski, L. A. *Behavioral habilitation through proactive programming*. Baltimore: Paul H. Brookes Publishing Co., 1981.

Bitter, J. A. *Introduction to rehabilitation*. St. Louis, MO: C. V. Mosby Co., 1979.

Borg, W. R., & Gall, M. D. *Educational research: An introduction* (2nd ed.). New York: David McKay Co., Inc., 1971.

Botterbusch, K. *A comparison of seven vocational evaluation systems*. Menomonie, WI: Materials Development Center, Stout Vocational Rehabilitation Institute, University of Wisconsin-Stout, 1976.

Botterbusch, K. *A comparison of four vocational evaluation systems*. Menomonie, WI: Materials Development Center, Stout Vocational Rehabilitation Institute, University of Wisconsin-Stout, 1977.

Botterbusch, K. *A comparison of commercial vocational evaluation systems*. Menomonie, WI: Materials Development Center, Stout Vocational Rehabilitation Institute, University of Wisconsin-Stout, 1980.

Brickey, M. Dexterity test utilization with moderately and severely retarded workshop employees. *Vocational Evaluation and Work Adjustment Bulletin*, 1982, *15*, 15–18.

Brolin, D. E. *Vocational preparation of retarded citizens*. Columbus, OH: Charles E. Merrill Publishing Co., 1976.

Brolin, D. E. *Vocational preparation of persons with handicaps*. Columbus, OH: Charles E. Merrill Publishing Co., 1982.

Dial, J., & Swearingen, S. The prediction of sheltered workshop performance: Special application of the McCarron-Dial work evaluation system. *Vocational Evaluation and Work Adjustment Bulletin*, 1976, *9*, 24–33.

Esser, T. J. *Client rating instruments for use in vocational rehabilitation agencies*. Menomonie, WI: Materials Development Center, Stout Vocational Rehabilitation Institute, University of Wisconsin-Stout, 1975.

Fortune, J., & Eldredge, G. Predictive validation of the McCarron-Dial evaluation system for psychiatrically disabled sheltered workshop workers. *Vocational Evaluation and Work Adjustment Bulletin*, 1982, 15, 136–141.

Gold, M. W. Research on the vocational rehabilitation of the retarded: The present, the future. In: N. R. Ellis (ed.), *International review of research in mental retardation*, Vol. 6. New York: Academic Press, 1973.

Johnson, J. L., & Mithaug, D. E. A replication survey of sheltered workshop entry requirements. *AAESPH Review*, 1978, *3*, 116–122.

Mehrens, W. A., & Lehmann, I. J. *Measurement and evaluation in education and psychology*. New York: Holt, Rinehart & Winston, 1973.

Mithaug, D. E. *Prevocational training for retarded students*. Springfield, IL: Charles C Thomas, 1981.

Mithaug, D. E., & Hagmeier, L. D. The development of procedures to assess prevocational competencies of severely handicapped young adults. *AAESPH Review*, 1978, *3*, 94–115.

Pruitt, W. A. *Vocational work evaluation*. Menonomie, WI: Walt Pruitt Associates, 1977.

Revell, W. G., Kriloff, L. J., & Sarkees, M.D. Vocational evaluation. In: P. Wehman & P. J. McLaughlin (eds.), *Vocational curriculum for developmentally disabled persons*. Baltimore: University Park Press, 1980.

Revell, W. G., & Wehman, P. Vocational evaluation of severely and profoundly retarded clients. *Rehabilitation Literature*, 1978, *39*, 226–231.

Rudrud, E. H., Ferrara, J. M., Wendelgass, P., Markve, R. A., & Decker, D. S. Community-referenced procedures for informing developmentally disabled clients about occupational training options. *Vocational Evaluation and Work Adjustment Bulletin*, 1982, *15*, 89–93.

Salvia, J., & Ysseldyke, J. E. *Assessment in special and remedial education*. Boston: Houghton Mifflin Co., 1981.

Schalock, R. L., & Karan, O. C. Relevant assessment: The interaction between evaluation and training. In: G. T. Bellamy, G. O'Connor, & O. C. Karan (eds.), *Vocational rehabilitation of severely handicapped persons*. Baltimore: University Park Press, 1979.

Schutz, R. P., & Rusch, F. R. Competitive employment: Toward employment integration for mentally retarded persons. In: K. P. Lynch, W. E. Kiernan, & J. A. Stark (eds.), *Prevocational and vocational education for special needs youth: A blueprint for the 1980s*. Baltimore: Paul H. Brookes Publishing Co., 1982.

Stodden, R. A., Casale, J., Schwartz, S. I. Work evaluation and the mentally retarded: Review and recommendations. *Mental Retardation*, 1977, *15*, 25–27.

Striefel, S., & Cadez, M. J. *Serving children and adolescents with developmental disabilities in the special education classroom: Proven methods*. Baltimore: Paul H. Brookes Publishing Co., 1983.

Timmerman, W. J., & Doctor, A. C. *Special applications of work evaluation techniques for prediction of employability of the trainable mentally retarded*. Menomonie, WI: Materials Development Center, Stout Vocational Rehabilitation Institute, University of Wisconsin-Stout, 1974.

APPENDIX:
TEST PUBLISHERS

Name of Test	Publisher
1. *Norm-Referenced Achievement Tests*	
Wide Range Achievement Test (WRAT)	Jastak Associates 1526 Gilpin Avenue Wilmington, DE 19806
Peabody Individual Achievement Test (PIAT)	American Guidance Service Publishers Building Circle Pines, MN 55014
Adult Basic Learning Examination (ABLE)	The Psychological Corporation 757 Third Avenue New York, NY 10017
2. *Criterion-Referenced Achievement Tests*	
SCAT Skill Screener	State Department of Education 650 West State Street Boise, ID 83720
Key Math Diagnostic Arithmetic Test	American Guidance Service Publishers Building Circle Pines, MN 55014
Brigance Diagnostic Inventory of Basic Skills	Curriculum Associates 94 Bridge Street Newton, MA 02158
3. *Vocational Aptitude Tests*	
General Aptitude Test Battery (GATB)	U.S. Government Printing Office Washington, DC 20402
Non-Reading Aptitude Test Battery (NATB)	U.S. Government Printing Office Washington, DC 20402
Differential Aptitude Tests	The Psychological Corporation 757 Third Avenue New York, NY 10017

4. *Motor Functioning and Manual Dexterity Tests*

Bennett Hand Tool Dexterity Test	The Psychological Corporation 757 Third Avenue New York, NY 10017
Purdue Pegboard	Science Research Associates 155 North Wacker Drive Chicago, IL 60606
Crawford Small Parts Dexterity Test	The Psychological Corporation 757 Third Avenue New York, NY 10017
O'Connor Finger and Tweezer Dexterity Tests	C. H. Stoelting 1350 S. Kostner Avenue Chicago, IL 60623
Stromberg Dexterity Test	The Psychological Corporation 757 Third Avenue New York, NY 10017
Bender Visual Motor Gestalt Test	The Psychological Corporation 757 Third Avenue New York, NY 10017

5. *Vocational Interest Inventories*

Strong-Campbell Interest Inventory	Stanford University Press Stanford, CA 94305
Kuder Occupational Interest Survey	Science Research Associates 155 North Wacker Drive Chicago, IL 60606
Geist Picture Interest Inventory	Western Psychological Services 12031 Wilshire Boulevard Los Angeles, CA 90025
Vocational Interest and Sophistication Assessment (VISA)	Dr. J. J. Parnick Nisonger Center The Ohio State University Columbus, OH 43210
Wide Range Interest-Opinion Test (WRIOT)	Jastak Associates 1526 Gilpin Avenue Wilmington, DE 19806
AAMD-Becker Reading-Free Vocational Interest Inventory	American Association on Mental Deficiency 3201 Connecticut Avenue, N.W. Washington, D.C. 20015

Reading-Free Vocational Interest Inventory   Elbern Publications
P.O. Box 09497
Columbus, OH 43209

6. *Work Samples*

TOWER System

I.C. Rehabilitation and
Research Center
340 East 24th Street
New York, NY 10010

Philadelphia Jewish Employment and
Vocational Service Work Sample System
(JEVS)

Vocational Research Institute
Jewish Employment and
Vocational Service
1700 Sawsom Street
Philadelphia, PA 19103

Vocational Information and Evaluation Work
Samples (VIEWS)

Vocational Research Institute
Jewish Employment and
Vocational Service
1700 Sawsom Street
Philadelphia, PA 19103

McCarron-Dial Work Evaluation System

McCarron-Dial Systems
P.O. Box 45628
Dallas, TX 75245

Valpar Component Work Sample Series

Valpar Corporation
3801 E. 34th Street
Tucson, AZ 85713

Pre-Vocational Readiness Battery

Valpar Corporation
3801 E. 34th Street
Tucson, AZ 85713

Wide Range Employment Sample Test
(WREST)

Jastak Associates
1526 Gilpin Avenue
Wilmington, DE 19806

7. *Client Rating Instruments*

AAMD Adaptive Behavior Scales

American Association on
Mental Deficiency
3201 Connecticut Avenue,
N.W.
Washington, D.C. 20015

MDC Behavior Identification Format

Materials Development
Center
Stout Vocational Rehabilita-
tion Institute
University of Wisconsin-
Stout
Menomonie, WI 54751

San Francisco Vocational Competency
Scale

The Psychological
Corporation
757 Third Avenue
New York, NY 10017

Work Adjustment Rating Form (WARF)

Dr. James A. Bitter
School of Special Education
   and Rehabilitation
University of Northern
   Colorado
Greeley, CO 80639

Prevocational Assessment and Curriculum
   Guide (PACG)

Exceptional Education
P.O. Box 15308
Seattle, WA 98115

Sioux Vocational School
   Social-Interpersonal Behavior Checklist

Materials Development
   Center
Stout Vocational Rehabilita-
   tion Institute
University of Wisconsin-
   Stout
Menomonie, WI 54751

CHAPTER 8

Community-Referenced Vocational Assessment

Chapter 7 raised serious questions regarding the value of most traditional vocational evaluation techniques with handicapped persons. The following deficiencies are particularly serious:

1. Many vocational assessment instruments lack reliability and validity data.
2. Many vocational assessment instruments are improperly utilized to keep handicapped persons out of competitive employment settings.
3. Many vocational assessment instruments do not reflect actual employment opportunities available within the local community.

A community-referenced assessment system can provide a proactive alternative to standardized vocational assessment. Such a system should be designed to answer four key questions:

1. What local job opportunities exist?
2. Which of the available jobs does the trainee prefer?
3. What elements of the preferred job can the trainee do and, conversely, on what elements of the job is training needed?
4. How well is the individual progressing toward acquiring the skills needed for the job?

SURVEY OF LOCAL JOB OPPORTUNITIES

The goal of vocational habilitation is full employment in an integrated setting. Thus, specific training goals and objectives must be based upon job opportunities available within the community into which the individual can be placed. Job opportunities may be identified by contacting job service offices, local businesses, business organizations, and civic organizations, as well as by reviewing classified ads and reviewing past placements.

Additional procedures used by Rusch and Mithaug (1980) included surveying employers by mail or telephone. In metropolitan and urban areas, telephone and mail surveys may be appropriate. For instance, Moss (1979) mailed letters with return postcards describing the food service training program and asked restaurant operators to respond if they were interested. Letters were sent to every third establishment listed in the Seattle Restaurant Owner's Guide. One hundred letters were mailed, but only eight cards were returned and no jobs were offered. The procedure that was found to be most effective was to send form letters to prospective employers explaining the program and inviting them to visit the training facility. The tour allowed the prospective employer to see the trainees at work in the kitchen and to see the similarities and differences between the training environment and the employer's establishment. Contact was then maintained with the prospective employer until a job opening occurred. Problems of job development diminished substantially after the first 2 years of this project, and once the project became known in the restaurant community, restaurant operators often called seeking employees. Thus, certain mail and telephone procedures can be very useful. However, they may not be needed in small towns and rural communities where most businesses can be personally contacted within a relatively brief period of time.

Regardless of how jobs are identified, all possible openings must be screened. This is necessary so that only jobs for which trainees will be eligible are included in your training program. Rudrud (1981) utilized the following criteria when screening jobs for disabled individuals:

1. The job should not require a high school diploma or have additional educational requirements.
2. The job should not require specialized certification or licensure (e.g., electrician, plumber, truck driver).
3. The job should not require experience.

JOB PREFERENCE

After local job opportunities have been identified, the next question to ask is which of the identified jobs do trainees prefer. The development of instrumentation to determine career interests and values of handicapped persons has lagged behind other approaches to work evaluation (Stodden & Ianacone, 1981). Reasons for this lag include: a) the perception that handicapped individuals are not serious candidates for competitive employment, b) attitudes that handicapped individuals cannot make valid career choices, and c) lack of appropriate preference assessment devices.

Standardized instruments are often useless in a small community where there are a limited number of jobs available within the community. Small communities do not offer as many job options as may be available in large communities. This is particularly problematic when using standardized vocational preference instruments. For example, the AAMD-Becker Reading-Free Vocational Interest Inventory (Becker, 1975) lists 11 male job categories and 8 female job categories. Rudrud (1981) collected job availability data in South Dakota and found 722 available jobs. However, 86% of those jobs were accounted for in only four AAMD-Becker categories. Thus, clients may indicate a preference for jobs in AAMD-Becker interest categories that do not exist in their community. Two characteristics of developmentally disabled individuals make this a particularly troublesome problem. First, developmently disabled individuals are likely to master fewer total jobs than the general population. Second, if a job that an individual wants and could be trained for is not available in his or her community, that person is not likely to be able to leave the community in search of such a position.

Additional problems in assessing vocational interests among mentally retarded individuals include: low reading ability, unrealistic fantasies about what tasks are required for various occupational titles, and lack of vocational experience. Many handicapped persons have limited knowledge about the nature of available jobs due to their nonexistent or limited work histories (Rudrud, Ferrara, Wendelgass, Markve, & Decker, 1982). This fact has implications in assessing vocational preference. It is unreasonable to ask people to state a preference for a job when they know nothing about it. The lack of vocational knowledge may result in guessing or making choices based upon serious misconceptions about jobs.

Ferrara, Rudrud, Wendelgass, and Markve (1983) asked trainees who had little job experience or training to indicate job preference by pointing to photo groups of job tasks. At first, it seemed that the trainees were making random choices. Later, analysis suggested that clients were making choices on the basis of irrelevant criteria. For example, some individuals chose only photographs that contained the color red. As a result, the preference inventory was invalid with a naive population. This indicates that it is important to acquaint a trainee with unfamiliar job experiences before asking that person to express a particular interest.

Assessing Preference

Two steps should be taken by staff to improve the validity and usefulness of job preference assessment. These steps are: 1) using appropriate assessment instruments, and 2) informing clients about behaviors required by available jobs. First of all, staff need to obtain or create a job preference inventory that accurately reflects jobs that are locally available. Standardized inventories may prove to be useful in a few very large communities where the jobs and training available match those measured by standardized preference inventories. In most cases, however, the use of such standardized inventories will be inappropriate. The instrument that surveys preferences for jobs that are not available and/or fails to survey preferences for jobs that are available is invalid. In most cases, the best way to procure a locally valid instrument is to create one.

The Huron Vocational Preference Inventory (HVPI) (Appendix A) is an example of a locally valid instrument. Each page of the nine-page inventory contains four photographs, one photograph for each of the four jobs identified in a survey of local opportunities. On each page, trainees are asked to point to the photograph of the specific job that they would like to do. After initially indicating their preference, they are then instructed to indicate their second, third, and fourth choices. Thus, each client rank-orders the four job tasks depicted on each page. The rankings for each of the four occupations are then totaled and the occupation with the lowest total reflects the client's vocational preference.

Once a preference inventory is developed, staff must inform clients about available jobs. This should be done *before* the administration of preference inventories so that trainees can make knowledgeable choices. Unless this is done, the results of even locally valid tests are likely to be meaningless (Ferrara et al., 1983).

Rudrud, Ferrara, Wendelgass, Markve, and Decker (1982) tested three techniques for informing clients about four job opportunities (auto detailing, janitorial service, maid service, and kitchen help). The three techniques included a slide/tape presentation, one-to-one discussion regarding locally available jobs, and one-to-one discussion utilizing a standardized job information manual.

Slide/Tape The slide/tape presentation consisted of 133 slides, and was approximately 11 minutes in duration (the script is shown in Appendix B). Each occupation was presented in the slide/tape in the following manner:

1. A statement indicating general responsibility was given (e.g., "The janitor is responsible for keeping offices and work spaces of buildings clean for the people who work there.").
2. Statements and visual slides depicting specific jobs performed were presented (e.g., "Janitors do many jobs, but most jobs are for floor care

such as sweeping, mopping, vacuuming, stripping and waxing the floor, and buffing.'').

3. Review questions such as, ''What are some of the jobs janitors do on floors?'' were asked. These were followed by a 3- to 5-second pause, after which the answer was given and accompanying slides were reviewed with the participant.

One-to-One Discussion Regarding Local Jobs One-to-one discussion was used to increase clients' vocational knowledge of the four occupations for which they could receive employment training. The discussion took approximately 10 minutes and was conducted by a staff member with whom the client was familiar. The staff member followed the script used in the slide/tape without pictures.

Control Treatment Control treatment was designed to approximate the discussion a client might be likely to receive in a normal vocational counseling situation; that is, without a systematic instructional program designed to inform clients about the jobs. The discussion script for this section was drawn largely from the South Dakota VIEW (Ritenour, 1982). The VIEW (Vital Information for Education and Work) is a directory designed to ''assist counselors and teachers in implementing vocational guidance programs'' (p. 2). One section of the VIEW materials includes brief job descriptions. Three of the jobs described in the VIEW (new car preparation mechanic, kitchen helper, and custodian) were roughly equivalent to the jobs taught via the methods described above. A brief general description of a motel maid's job was also included. This discussion took approximately 5 minutes and was delivered by a staff member with whom the client was familiar. Following the reading of the standard script, the staff member answered any questions the trainee had about the four occupations.

Which Training Program Should We Use?

Results of the Huron Vocational Knowledge Test (Appendix C) indicated that the most effective training approach was the slide/tape program. This program effectively taught both high and low IQ trainees about the four jobs. Furthermore, when these trainees took the HVPI, their ranking of the individual pictures was based upon job-related factors rather than irrelevant variables such as color.

For some trainees with high verbal ability, one-to-one discussion proved to be equally effective. However, this method was not as effective with low IQ/low verbal ability trainees. This procedure has the advantage of being less expensive than the slide/tape and may, therefore, be attractive to agencies serving relatively high functioning trainees.

The standardized job manual could be considered worse than ineffective. This procedure failed to teach either high or low functioning trainees very much specific information about the four jobs. At the same time, this procedure introduced a marked sex bias about the jobs. Trainees exposed to this material made HVPI rankings on the basis of the sex of the model in the pictures, not the jobs the models were performing.

Exercises

8-1. List the four questions that are important in community-referenced evaluation.
8-2. List key activities for identifying local jobs.
8-3. List the procedures for identifying job preference if no commercially available instrument is referenced to your community.

Answers to Exercises

8-1. What local job opportunities exist? Which of the available jobs does the trainee prefer? What elements of the preferred jobs can the trainee do? How well is the individual progressing?
8-2. Survey past placements, contact job service, survey local businesses, review classified ads, contact business and civic organizations, use mail and telephone contacts.
8-3. Identify local jobs, develop a way to inform clients about the job, have clients rank photos of different parts of the available jobs.

ABILITY TO DO THE JOB

For any assessment of vocational competence to be useful to trainers, two important criteria must be met: a) test items must accurately reflect the task requirement found in actual job placements, and b) there must be a clear relationship between test items and the training to be provided to the trainee. The first task of individuals wishing to develop community-referenced assessments of vocational skills is to list the tasks required of people doing specific jobs.

Two types of validation used to identify job skills (descriptive and comparative validation) (Schutz & Rusch, 1982), were described in Chapter 2. Descriptive reports consist of interviews or surveys that request employers and/or supervisors to identify behaviors they judge to be important. For example, in auto detailing, is it important for the worker to be able to drive the car into the cleaning area? If so, the worker needs to be taught how to drive, or an alternative arrangement needs to be found (e.g., supervisor moves cars).

The second type of validation is comparative validation, which involves observing workers actually performing the target job. This approach can prevent a problem that would have arisen if descriptive reports were relied upon solely; disparities may exist between what employers say are important skills and what, in fact, are critical skills for success (Schutz & Rusch, 1982). For example, employers may state that workers should be able to read when in fact the job may only require that workers stack boxes "this end up." Thus, the worker does not necessarily have to read, but rather stack boxes so that the correct end is up.

Figure 8.1 shows the skill lists developed using these procedures for the four jobs identified by the Huron Area Adjustment Training Center.

Competitive Standards

Skills lists alone do not adequately describe expected performance. A major concern of employers is that the worker can perform a job at competitive standards (e.g., rate, accuracy). Thus, for each skill, a specific competitive standard needs to be identified. Standards relating to accuracy and rate can be identified by watching a skilled person perform the job. Competitive rates, however, are best determined through time studies (Dunn, 1977; Iverson, 1978).

There are various methods that can be used to establish time standards. The preferred technique is to identify workers in industry who are performing the job and measure their rates of production. Worker production rates can then be compared with industrial standards. This procedure was used to establish standards for the auto detailing component of the training program at the Huron Adjustment Training Center. Staff were asked to complete job tasks so that time standards could be calculated. The staff then met with potential employers and asked the employers if the times identified were appropriate. For example, two staff washed and vacuumed cars. It took between 45 and 60 minutes to complete all tasks involved. The staff then asked the automobile dealer if this was considered an acceptable rate. The automobile dealer indicated that this was an acceptable rate and that he would hire an individual who could complete the job at those rates. This technique was also used to develop norms for the janitorial program.

Development of Test Items

Once a list of job behaviors has been validated and competitive standards established, test developers must find ways to determine which job skills or components of those skills trainees have acquired. These component skills are often described in teaching task analyses. (The teaching task analyses for Huron's auto detailing domain are provided in Appendix D.) Test items may be developed from either the skills list or from relatively difficult substeps on the teaching task analyses. In any case, test items should meet the following criteria:

1. Test items should be directly tied to a step on either skill list or teaching task analysis.
2. Specific written directions should be provided to persons administering the test.
3. Specific criteria should be provided for judging whether the response made by the trainee is correct. These criteria should be the same as either

I. Janitorial skills
   A. Floor care
      1. Sweep floor
      2. Mop floor
      3. Vacuum floor
      4. Dust mop floor
      5. Buff floor
      6. Strip floor
      7. Neutralize floor
      8. Seal floor
      9. Wax floor
      10. Spot clean rugs and door mats
      11. Clean steps
   B. Clean restrooms
      1. Clean mirrors and windows
      2. Clean sinks and hardware
      3. Clean toilet bowls, seats, and urinals
      4. Spot clean stainless steel (grab bars, push/kick plates, plumbing hardware, drinking fountains)
      5. Spot clean walls/partitions
      6. Unclog sinks and toilets
      7. Sweep floor
      8. Mop floor
      9. Empty wastebaskets
      10. Refill dispensers—toilet paper, towels, soap
   C. Clean offices
      1. Empty wastebaskets
      2. Empty ashtrays
      3. Dust furniture
      4. Clean windows and mirrors
      5. Vacuum floor
      6. Dust mop
      7. Mop floor
      8. Buff floor
   D. Clean break areas
      1. Sweep floor
      2. Empty ashtrays
      3. Empty wastebaskets
      4. Dust furniture
      5. Clean table tops
      6. Clean counters
      7. Clean sink
      8. Wipe appliances
      9. Clean windows
      10. Mop floor

      11. Buff floor
      12. Refill dispensers
   E. Clean hallways
      1. Sweep floor
      2. Empty trash
      3. Empty ashtrays
      4. Mop floor
      5. Buff floor
      6. Vacuum floor
      7. Clean windows
      8. Spot clean walls
      9. Clean drinking fountain
   F. Special tasks
      1. Clean janitorial equipment/closet
      2. Replace mop heads
      3. Replace broom heads
      4. Replace light bulbs (regular)
      5. Replace light bulbs (fluorescent)
      6. Remove gum
      7. Lock doors (key lock)
      8. Lock doors (button lock)
      9. Unlock doors
      10. Arrange table/chair set ups
II. Maid service skills
   A. Restock supply cart with:
      1. Cleaning supplies
      2. Trash bag
      3. Dirty linen bag
      4. Room supplies—soap, glasses, matches
      5. Clean towels
      6. Clean linen
   B. Clean room
      1. Enter room/hang "Do not disturb" sign
      2. Check lights
      3. Turn on lamp
      4. Pick up trash
      5. Empty ashtrays
      6. Open drapes
      7. Dust furniture
   C. Make the bed
      1. Strip bed
      2. Make bed
   D. Vacuum floor
   E. Clean bathroom
      1. Sweep, vacuum, or wash floor
      2. Clean tub, tub wall, and shower curtain
      3. Clean sink and vanity

(continued)

Figure 8.1. Job skills validated for Huron, South Dakota.

4. Clean mirror
5. Clean toilet
6. Replenish bathroom supplies—soap, glasses, tissue
7. Refill dispensers
F. Special tasks
  1. Change light bulbs
  2. Change bathroom lights with fixtures
III. Auto detail skills
A. Auto detail supply check
B. Prepare car for cleaning
C. Wash car
D. Rinse car
E. Wipe car

F. Clean car windows and mirrors
G. Vacuum car
H. Operate car buffer/polisher
I. Clean work area
IV. Kitchen helper skills
A. Operate dishwasher
B. Load dish trays
C. Unload clean trays
D. Load silverware
E. Turn dishwasher off
F. Wash pots and utensils
G. Sweep floor
H. Mop floor
I. Empty wastebaskets
J. Clean work area

Figure 8.1. (*continued*)

worksite standards or intermediate standards set forth in the training task analysis.

4. The tools and materials used should be similar to the tools and materials available in the competitive work setting. For example, in waxing cars, one does not apply wax by hand; rather, a car buffer is used.

An appropriate test item for the first step of the auto detailing skill list is shown in Figure 8.2.

Use of Test Results

Records of trainee performance on the type of test item described in Figure 8.2 may be used in three ways: a) as an entry level pretest, b) as an exit level posttest, and c) as an ongoing measure of individual progress.

Prior to beginning instruction, trainers should determine what tasks and/or component skills the trainee can already do. This addresses the proactive question, "Where are you?" Following instruction, the same test items can be used to confirm for both trainees and employers that workers can do the job. It is important to note that, unlike many standardized vocational assessment devices, this kind of test may be given daily without affecting its validity. In this situation, "teaching to the test" is encouraged because the behaviors needed to pass the test are precisely the behaviors needed to do the job.

Finally, since test items may be given daily, they may be used as measures of individual progress toward acquiring the overall skill. The results of a trainee's performance over 5 days of instruction in car wash material identification are shown in Figures 8.3 and 8.4. Many proactive facilities utilize tabular data recording procedures as an alternative to the charting shown in Figure 8.4. Figure 8.5 depicts the client data above in tabular form.

Daily data are useful since they allow trainers to judge the effectiveness of training as well as provide direction in correcting trainee errors. In addition,

Objective: If supplies are not present, the trainee will report this absence to the supervisor.

Directions: Have all but five of the items listed below available in the shop.

Say: "Check to see if what you need is here."
(Wait 10 seconds)
Say: "Is anything missing?"
(After the student responds correctly, continue).
Say: "If this happens at work, what should you do?"
Write: A list of any missing items that the trainee does not report.

Correct response:

1. The student should say what is missing within 5 seconds.
2. The student should say, "I tell _____ (name of supervisor)."

Repeat three times with 15 different missing items

Tire cleaner	Pressure wand
Clean cloth towels	Car soap
Newspapers	Rags
Paper towels	Solvent (tar/bug)
Basket	Trash can
Vacuum cleaner	Dirty laundry bag
Window cleaner	Wringer (electric)
Scrub brush	Broom

Figure 8.2. Sample vocational skills test item.

Day	Number of items reported	Items reported or not reported (whichever is less)
4/1	3/15	Reported: tire cleaner, pressure wand, scrub brush
4/2	8/15	Reported: tire cleaner, clean cloth towels, pressure wand, scrub brush, car soap, solvent, trash can, broom
4/3	10/15	Not reported: dirty laundry bag, rags, window cleaner, basket, vacuum cleaner
4/4	13/15	Not reported: window cleaner, vacuum cleaner
4/5	15/15	

Figure 8.3. Data on materials identification.

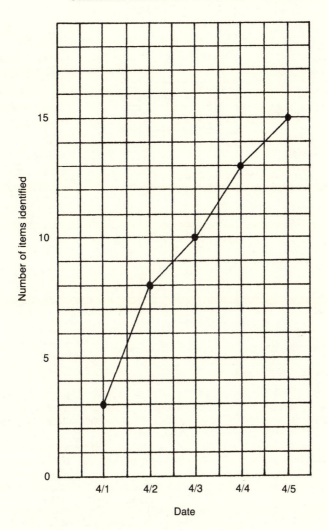

Figure 8.4. Graphed data on materials identified.

data that are charted daily often appear to be effective reinforcement for both trainers and trainees.

Exercises

8-4. List the characteristics of community-referenced test items.
8-5. How can trainers use a community-referenced job performance test?
8-6. How do traditional evaluation procedures and community-referenced evaluation procedures differ in the areas of job skills covered, vocational preferences, measuring job performance, and usefulness to the trainer?

| Check for: | Dates | | | | | Scoring summary: |
	4/1	4/2	4/3	4/4	4/5	
Clean cloth towels	0	3	3	3	3	3—without assistance
Newspapers	0	0	3	3	3	2—verbal prompt
Paper towels	0	0	3	3	3	1—gestural/imitation
Basket	0	0	0	3	3	0—physical prompt or
Vacuum cleaner	0	1	1	1	3	no response
Window cleaner	0	1	1	1	3	N+—not tested
Pressure wand	3	3	3	3	3	
Car soap	0	3	3	3	3	
Rags	0	0	0	3	3	
Solvent (tar/bug)	0	3	3	3	3	
Trash can	0	3	3	3	3	
Dirty laundry bag	0	0	0	3	3	
Wringer (electric)	N+	N+	N+	N+	N+	
Broom	0	3	3	3	3	
Scrub brush	3	3	3	3	3	
Tire cleaner	3	3	3	3	3	

Figure 8.5. Tabular data on materials identification.

Answers to Exercises

8-4. They should be directly tied to items on the skill list and/or to component skills, they should be written and provide specific instructions for people doing the assessment, they should provide specific criteria for scoring, and the tools and materials should be similar to those in competitive settings.

8-5. Trainers can use a community-referenced job performance test as an entry level pretest, as an exit level posttest, and as an ongoing measure of individual progress.

8-6.

		Community-referenced evaluation	Traditional vocational evaluation
1.	Job skills	Based upon locally available jobs	Based upon general vocational skill areas
2.	Vocational preference	Surveys clients only on those jobs that are available	Surveys clients on a wide variety of jobs
3.	Job performance	Identifies specific skills a person can and cannot do; these skills are directly related to local job training programs	Measures behavior that may or may not be related to available jobs
4.	Usefulness to trainer	Tells the trainer precisely where to begin instruction; often can provide a basis for daily progress evaluation	Rarely identifies remedial steps to assist in programming

SUMMARY

Community-referenced vocational assessment should answer the following questions:

1. What local job opportunities exist?
2. Which of the available jobs does the trainee prefer?
3. What elements of the preferred job can the trainee do and, conversely, on what elements of the job is training needed?
4. How well is the individual progressing toward acquiring the skills needed for the job?

SUGGESTED ACTIVITIES

1. Review your agency's past job placements. Note how many placements occur in each job category.
2. Obtain a list of job openings from job service and/or the local paper. Find those jobs that do not require: a) previous experience, b) a special license, and c) a high school, GED, or college degree.
3. How does your agency currently assess: a) local job opportunities, b) job preference, c) the elements of a job that an individual can do, and d) how well an individual is progressing in acquiring necessary skills?
4. Discuss with your colleagues the differences between your agency's approach to vocational assessment and the approach described in this chapter.

REFERENCES

Becker, R. L. *AAMD-Becker Reading-Free Vocational Interest Inventory*. Washington, DC: American Association on Mental Deficiency, 1975.

Dunn, D.J. *Using competitive norms and industrial standards with work samples*. Menomonie, WI: Research and Training Center, Stout Vocational Rehabilitation Institute, 1977.

Ferrara J., Rudrud, E., Wendelgass, P., & Markve, R. *The effect of vocational knowledge training upon the vocational preference of mentally retarded adults*. In preparation, 1983.

Iverson, S. *Time study techniques*. Salt Lake City, UT: Columbus Community Center, 1978.

Moss, J.W. *Post secondary vocational education for mentally retarded adults*. Reston, VA: Council for Exceptional Children, 1979.

Ritenour, C. *South Dakota VIEW*. Pierre, SD: Division of Vocational Education, 1982.

Rudrud, E. Job openings and client placements: Over and under-met needs. *Vocational Evaluation and Work Adjustment Bulletin, 1981, 14*, 80–82.

Rudrud, E., Ferrara, J., Wendelgass, P., Markve, R.A., & Decker, D. Community-referenced procedures for informing developmentally disabled clients about occupational training options. *Vocational Evaluation and Work Adjustment Bulletin, 1982, 15*, 89–93.

Rudrud, E., Wendelgass, P., Markve, R.A., Ferrara, J.A., & Decker, D. S. Community-referenced assessment of vocational knowledge and preference. *Vocational Evaluation and Work Adjustment Bulletin, 1982, 15*, 19–21.

Rusch, F.R., & Mithaug, D.E. *Vocational training for mentally retarded adults.* Champaign, IL: Research Press, 1980.

Schutz, R.P., & Rusch, F.R. Competitive employment: Toward employment integration for mentally retarded persons. IN: K.P. Lynch, W.E. Kiernan, & J.A. Stark (eds.), *Prevocational and vocational education for special needs youth: A blueprint for the 1980s.* Baltimore: Paul H. Brookes Publishing Co., 1982.

Stodden, R.A., & Ianacone, R.N. Career/vocational assessment of the special needs individual: A conceptual model. *Exceptional Children,* 1981, *47,* 600–608.

APPENDIX A

HURON VOCATIONAL ASSESSMENT PROGRAM
VOCATIONAL PREFERENCE INVENTORY

Instructions

The Vocational Preference Assessment Test is comprised of photographs of the various job tasks associated with the four occupations depicted in the slide/tape presentation. There are nine pages in the Vocational Preference Assessment Test. Each page consists of four photographs; one photograph from each of the four occupations. The client rank-orders each photograph on each page by indicating which job he or she would like to do. This test can be used in a pre-posttest fashion with the slide/tape presentation.

Administration

On each page are four photographs showing various job tasks associated with the four occupations. In the corner of each photograph is a letter indicating that the photograph represents: A = auto detailing, J = janitorial service, M = maid sevice, and K = kitchen help.

Each page is presented to the client, and the examiner should say, "Point to the picture of the job that you would like to do." The client's response is then recorded on the score sheet by placing a "1," indicating first choice, in the appropriate column. The examiner then says, "If you could not do that job, which job would you like to do?" The client's response is then recorded on the score sheet by placing a "2" in the appropriate column, indicating the client's second choice. The examiner then repeats the procedure requiring the client to indicate his or her third choice. The picture that has not been pointed to is scored as "4" and the examiner can turn the page to the next set of four photographs. On each page, the examiner asks the client to indicate his or her first, second, third, and fourth choice of jobs that he or she would like to do.

Scoring

Following are examples of a blank and a completed score sheet.

Huron Vocational Assessment Program
Vocational Preference

Name _____ Administered by _____

Date _____

Page	Auto detailing	Janitorial service	Maid service	Kitchen helper
1	_____	_____	_____	_____
2	_____	_____	_____	_____
3	_____	_____	_____	_____
4	_____	_____	_____	_____
5	_____	_____	_____	_____
6	_____	_____	_____	_____
7	_____	_____	_____	_____
8	_____	_____	_____	_____
9	_____	_____	_____	_____
TOTAL	==========	==========	==========	==========

The rank order for each occupation is totaled and the occupation with the lowest rank indicates the client's vocational preference. Second and third preferences can also be computed.

First preference (lowest score) _____

Second preference _____

Third preference _____

Fourth preference (highest score) _____

Huron Vocational Assessment Program
Vocational Preference

Name _____ Administered by _____

Date _____

Page	Auto detailing	Janitorial service	Maid service	Kitchen helper
1	1	2	4	3
2	1	2	4	3
3	2	1	4	3
4	2	3	4	1
5	1	3	4	2
6	1	3	4	2
7	1	2	4	3
8	2	2	4	3
9	1	2	3	4
TOTAL	12	20	35	24

The rank order for each occupation is totaled and the occupation with the lowest rank indicates the client's vocational preference. Second and third preferences can also be computed.

First preference (lowest score)	Auto detailing
Second preference	Janitorial service
Third preference	Kitchen helper
Fourth preference (highest score)	Maid sevice

Huron Vocational Assessment Program
Vocational Preference Inventory

Photographs Used

Page	Positions 1	2	3	4
1	Rinsing car (title slide)	Janitor buffing floor (title slide)	Washing pots/ pans (title slide)	Maid meeting with supervisor (title slide)
2	Maid cleaning shower	Preparing car for washing (rolling up windows)	Janitor sweeping floor	Scraping dirty trays
3	Rinsing trays	Maid removing dirty towels	Spraying car	Janitor mopping floor
4	Janitor vacuuming floor	Loading trays into dishwasher	Placing clean towels in bathroom	Washing car with soapy water
5	Rinsing car	Janitor waxing floor	Operating dishwasher	Maid stripping bed
6	Making bed	Drying (wiping car)	Buffing floor	Stacking clean dishes
7	Washing pots and pans	Maid dusting furniture	Cleaning car windows	Janitor cleaning mirror
8	Janitor dusting furniture	Kitchen helper wiping counter	Maid vacuuming floor	Vacuuming car
9	Waxing car with car buffer	Janitor changing light bulbs	Kitchen helper mopping floor	Maid leaving clean glasses and soap

APPENDIX B

(Numbers on script refer to slides)

Note: Start slide/tape on black slide.[1]

HURON VOCATIONAL ASSESSMENT PROGRAM[2]
SLIDE/TAPE PRESENTATION

Sometimes it's hard to get a job.[3] People often read their local newspapers to find a job that they can do.[4] But not everyone can do every job that is listed. Many people need more training to learn how to do a new job.

This is Huron Area Adjustment Training Center.[5] The staff at Huron Area[6] Adjustment Training Center provide job training to help people get jobs. The staff train people to get important jobs in auto detailing,[7] janitorial service,[8] maid[9] service, and kitchen help.[10] Try to remember these jobs so that you can choose one you want to learn to do.

The first job is auto detailing.[11] Auto detailers work at car lots.[12] They are responsible for keeping the cars clean. The first thing you do is check with the[13] supervisor to find out which cars and trucks need to be cleaned.

To begin cleaning the car, auto detailers prepare the car by closing the[14] windows, unlocking the doors, removing floor mats, and putting the radio antenna down.

The next step is to wet the car.[15] Wetting the car helps to loosen dirt so that the car is easier to wash. After the car is wet, you wash the car by rubbing the entire[16] car with soapy water. When the car is completely washed, you rinse it.[17] The car must be rinsed until all the soap is gone. The next step is to dry the car.[18] You use clean, dry towels to wipe all the water from the car. Each car window is then[19] cleaned with a spray cleaner. After the windows are cleaned, you must check for[20] any remaining dirt or water spots.[21] When the outside of the car is clean, the inside of the car and the floor mats are vacuumed.

After the car is cleaned, it is waxed.[22] To wax a car, you use a car buffer.[23] The

133

first step is to put the wax on the car with the car [24] buffer. After the wax is dry, you [25] use the buffer to remove the wax. After the [26] wax is removed, you polish the [27] car with a polishing pad on the car buffer.

[28] Let's stop a minute and review the jobs that an auto detailer does. Can you name a place where an auto detailer works? Auto [29] detailers work at car lots.

Can you name the jobs an auto detailer does? An auto detailer prepares [30] the car, [31] wets down the car, [32] washes the car, [33] rinses the car, [34] dries the car, [35] cleans car windows, checks the outside of the [36] car for water spots, and vacuums the [37] inside of the car and the floor mats. After [38] the car is cleaned, the car can be waxed with a car buffer. It's nice to see a job well done [39] and to turn a dirty car into a [40] clean one.

Another job that you can learn at Huron Adjustment Training Center [41] is janitorial work. Janitorial work is important work [42] in public buildings, schools, and offices. The janitor is responsible for keeping [43] offices and workspaces of buildings clean for the people who work there.

[44] The janitor gets work assignments from the maintenance supervisor. Janitors do many jobs, but most jobs are for floor care [45] such as sweeping, [46] mopping, [47] vacuuming, [48] stripping and waxing the floor, and [49] buffing. Janitors also [50] dust [51] furniture, clean restrooms, [52] empty trash, and perform [53] minor building maintenance jobs like changing lightbulbs. [54] When restroom supplies are low, janitors restock used supplies with new ones. [55] Janitorial work is important work and when janitors clean offices they must be honest and careful with the property in the offices.

[56] Let's pause for a moment and think about the things that janitors do. Where do janitors work? In public [57] buildings and offices. What are some of the jobs that janitors do on floors? They [58] sweep, [59] mop, [60] vacuum, [61] strip and wax the floor, and buff [62] the floor. What are some of the other jobs that janitors do? They dust [63] furniture, [64] clean restrooms, [65] empty trash, [66] perform minor building maintenance jobs, and [67] restock used supplies.

[68] Another job that you can learn at Huron Area Adjustment Training Center is maid service. [69] Maids work in hotels and motels. Maids are very important to motels because maids are responsible for [70] cleaning the guest's room. Maids report to the supervisor to finds out which motel rooms need to be cleaned. [71] The maid's job centers around the supply cart. [72] The supply cart carries cleaning [73] materials and

clean linen including clean washcloths, towels, sheets, and pillowcases. The [74] supply cart also has a place to store dirty sheets, pillowcases, dirty towels and [75] washcloths, and trash.

A maid has many jobs to do. [76] The maid begins by cleaning the bathroom [77] including the sink, shower, and toilet. [78] The maid then picks up the dirty towels and [79] washcloths and puts clean towels and washcloths in the bathroom. [80] The maid then picks up all the trash from the room, [81] changes the dirty sheets and pillow [82] cases from the bed, and makes the bed with clean sheets. [83] The maid also dusts the furniture, [84] vacuums the floor, [85] and leaves clean glasses and soap for the [86] guests. It is important for a maid to be honest and take pride in the work being done. [87] The guests depend on the maid for the safety of their possessions and the cleanliness of their rooms.

Let's stop a moment and think about maid service. [88] Do you remember where maids work? [89] Maids work at hotels and motels. What jobs do maids do? [90] They clean bathrooms, [91] pick up dirty towels and washcloths, put clean towels and [92] washcloths in the bathroom, pick up trash from the room, [93] change dirty sheets and [94] pillowcases, [95] put clean sheets on the beds, dust furniture, [96] vacuum the floor, [97] and leave clean glasses and soap for the guest. [98]

The last job that you can learn at Huron Area Adjustment Training Center is [99] being a kitchen helper. Kitchen helpers work in restaurants and cafeterias. [100] Kitchen helpers are responsible for keeping dishes, utensils, pots, and pans [101] clean. Kitchen helpers report to their supervisor who tells them what to do. [102] A kitchen helper may do many things. When dirty dishes are brought to the kitchen, [103] the kitchen helper must scrape the dishes, [104] rinse the dishes, and put them [105] into dishwasher trays. When the dishwasher trays are full, [106] they are loaded into the dishwasher. The kitchen helper must then operate the dishwasher [107] until the dishes are clean. When the dishwasher is done, [108] the kitchen helper must remove the clean dishes and then stack and store the dishes in their proper places. [109] Kitchen helpers must also wash pots and pans by hand to be sure they get clean. [110] Other jobs that kitchen helpers must do are washing counters and tables, [111] sweeping and mopping floors, [112] and taking out garbage. [113]

Let's stop and review the jobs that a kitchen helper does. [114] Do you remember

where a kitchen helper works? Kitchen helpers work at restaurants and cafe-[115]
terias. What kinds of jobs do kitchen helpers do? They scrape and rinse dishes,[116]
put dishes into trays,[117] load the trays into the dishwasher,[118] operate the dishwasher,[119]
remove clean dishes,[120] stack and store dishes,[121] wash pots and pans by hand,[122] wash[123]
counters and tables,[124] sweep and mop floors,[125] and take out garbage.

It's time to look back at what we have learned.[126] The Huron Area Adjustment
Training Center is here to help you prepare for a new and important job in auto[127]
detailing,[128] janitorial work,[129] maid service,[130] or kitchen help. Each job occurs in a
special place and has special tasks for you to learn.

One of these jobs is best for you.[131] We hope you will be able to select a new
and important job that you would like to do.

Credit[132]

Credit[133]

APPENDIX C

HURON VOCATIONAL ASSESSMENT PROGRAM
VOCATIONAL KNOWLEDGE TEST

Instructions

The vocational knowledge test of the Huron Vocational Assessment Program is designed to measure an individual's knowledge of general and specific job tasks engaged in by each occupation. The vocational knowledge test was designed to be used as a pre/posttest accompanied by the slide/tape program.

Administration

Each test item is to be asked of the individual taking the test. It is permissible to repeat the test item *once* if the individual makes no response or asks for the question to be repeated.

Test items 2, 5, 8, 11, and 14 require the individual to list multiple answers. On these test items, the examiner should review the individual's response to the previous question and repeat the test item. For example:

Examiner: "What jobs do janitors do?"
Individual: "They sweep, wax floors, and buff."
Examiner: "I asked you what jobs do janitors do and you told me that janitors sweep floors, wax floors, and buff floors. Now, can you tell me other jobs that janitors do?"
Individual: "Yeah, they clean bathrooms and change light bulbs."

Scoring

On each test sheet, there is a column to indicate which items the individual answered correctly. There are a total of 49 correct responses on the vocational knowledge test. Correct responses are indicated on the test sheet. Several scoring rules should be followed.

1. *Similar wording is scored as correct.* Individuals who take the test are going to vary in their verbal abilities, and, as long as the general idea is communicated, the item is scored correct. For example:

   "A maid makes the bed with clean sheets." One individual stated that a maid changes the linen. This was scored as correct. "A kitchen helper operates the dishwasher." One individual stated that he or she pushes a button, which was a correct response. "A janitor works in public buildings, schools, and offices." One individual responded that a janitor works at the federal building. "A kitchen helper works in restaurants and cafeterias." One individual responded that a kitchen helper works at The Barn, which was the name of a local restaurant.

2. *Identifying one concept of a two-concept answer is scored as correct.* Several job concepts were presented in the slide/tape as a single job, and if the individual identifies one of the two concepts presented, then the entire concept is credited as being correct. For example, the slide/tape presen-

tation notes that "janitors strip and wax floors." These operations were similar and presented as one concept rather than two distinct operations and therefore, if an individual states that janitors "wax floors," then the answer "strip and wax floors" is credited as being correct.

Huron Vocational Assessment Program
Vocational Knowledge Test

1. What do the staff at Huron ATC do?
   Help/train people to get jobs ____
2. What are the four jobs that Huron ATC staff can train you to do?
   Auto detailing ____
   Janitorial service ____
   Maid service ____
   Kitchen helper ____
3. Where do auto detailers work?
   Auto dealerships/car lots ____
4. What are auto detailers responsible for?
   Washing or cleaning cars/keeping cars clean ____
5. How does an auto detailer clean cars?
   Prepares car/rolls up windows ____
   Wets down car ____
   Washes car/rubs car with soapy water ____
   Rinses the car ____
   Dries the car ____
   Cleans the car's windows ____
   Checks for spots/cleans mirrors ____
   Vacuums inside of car ____
   Waxes the car ____
6. Where do janitors work?
   Buildings, schools, offices ____
7. What are janitors responsible for?
   Keeping buildings, offices, and workspaces clean ____
8. What jobs do janitors do?
   Sweep floors ____
   Mop floors ____
   Vacuum ____
   Strip and wax floors ____
   Buff the floor ____
   Dust furniture ____
   Clean restrooms ____
   Refill supplies/towels in dispenser ____

Empty trash ____

Minor building maintenance/change lightbulbs ____

9. Where do maids work?

Motels/hotels ____

10. What are maids responsible for?

Cleaning rooms/making guests comfortable ____

11. What jobs do maids do?

Remove trash from room ____

Pick up dirty sheets/pillowcases ____

Make bed with clean sheets ____

Pick up dirty towels/washcloths ____

Put clean towels/washcloths in bathroom ____

Clean bathroom ____

Leave clean glasses and soap ____

Dust furniture ____

Vacuum the floor ____

12. Where do kitchen helpers work?

Restaurants and cafeterias ____

13. What are kitchen helpers responsible for?

Keeping dishes, utensils, and pots/pans clean ____

14. What jobs do kitchen helpers do?

Scrape and rinse dishes ____

Load dishes into trays ____

Put trays in/operate dishwasher ____

Remove clean dishes from dishwasher ____

Stack and store clean dishes ____

Wash pots and pans ____

Wash counters and tables ____

Sweep/mop floors ____

Take out garbage ____

TOTAL ____

APPENDIX D
AUTO DETAIL TASK ANAYLSIS

Auto detail (supply check)
Prepare car for cleaning
Wash car
Rinse car
Wipe car
Clean car windows and mirrors
Vacuum car
Wax and polish car
Clean work area

[Task analyses for these eight steps appear on the following pages.]

Task Analysis Data Sheet

Program __Auto detail (supply check)__

Client _____

Instructor _____

Reinforcers _____

Materials _____

Task statement "_____"

Scoring summary:

3—without assistance

2—verbal prompt

1—gestural/imitative

0—physical prompt

	Dates									
1. Check to see if all cleaning material supplies are present										
2. Check for: tire cleaner										
3. clean cloth towels										
4. newspapers										
5. paper towels										
6. basket										
7. vacuum cleaner										
8. window cleaner										
9. pressure wand										
10. car soap										
11. rags										
12. solvent (tar/bug)										
13. trash can										
14. dirty laundry bag										
15. wringer (electric)										
16. broom										
17. scrub brush										
18. If supplies not present, report to supervisor										
19.										
20.										
21.										
22.										
23.										
24.										
25.										
Number of steps scored 3:										

Task Analysis Data Sheet

Program ___Prepare car for cleaning___

Client _____

Instructor _____

Reinforcers _____

Materials _____

Task statement "_____"

Scoring summary

3—without assistance

2—verbal prompt

1—gestural/imitative

0—physical prompt

Dates

1. Open car door										
2. Unlock all locked doors (if electric, turn on key)										
3. Roll up windows (if electric, turn on key)										
4. Take out floor mats										
5. Take out any personal possessions and place them in a box										
6. Close doors										
7. If car has floor mats, gather all floor mats										
8. Hang on 2″ × 4″ spring clamps										
9.										
10.										
11.										
12.										
13.										
14.										
15.										
16.										
17.										
18.										
19.										
20.										
21.										
22.										
23.										
24.										
25.										
Number of steps scored 3:										

Task Analysis Data Sheet

Program __Wash car__

Client _____

Instructor _____

Reinforcers _____

Materials _____

Task statement "_____"

Scoring summary

3—without assistance

2—verbal prompt

1—gestural/imitative

0—physical prompt

	Dates								
1. Go to cleaning shelf									
2. Get brush and bucket									
3. Get soap (1 quart container)									
4. Unscrew soap cap									
5. Pour 2 capfuls of soap into bucket									
6. Replace cap on soap									
7. Replace soap on shelf									
8. Carry bucket to spray gun or hose									
9. Pick up spray gun handle with preferred hand									
10. Point gun in bucket									
11. Turn on switch									
12. Fill bucket ¾ of the way to the top									
13. Point gun at car mats and soak									
14. Turn mats over									
15. Spray mats									
16. Move gun to middle of left side of car									
17. Spray one half of the roof (near side, lengthwise)									
18. Spray near side of car, top to bottom									
19. Spray front windshield									
20. Spray hood									
21. Spray grill									
22. Spray right side of car, top to bottom, including unsprayed half of roof									
23. Spray rear of car, top to bottom									
24. Spray rear bumper									
25. Turn gun off									

(continued)

Dates

26. Carry bucket and brush to mats											
27. Brush mat											
28. Turn mat over											
29. Brush second side of mat											
30. Repeat #27–29 for all mats											
31. Take bucket and brush to one of tires											
32. Wash all four tires with brush											
33. Move to middle of left side of car with bucket, rag, and sponge											
34. Wash near half of the roof											
35. Wash left side of car											
36. Wash front windshield (near side)											
37. Wash hood (near side)											
38. Wash front windshield (far side)											
39. Wash hood (far side)											
40. Wash grill and bumper (use brush and solvent for bugs)											
41. Wash right side of car including unwashed half of roof, top to bottom											
42. Wash right rear side of car top to bottom											
43. Wash left rear side of car top to bottom											
44. Wash rear bumper using solvent for bugs											
45.											
46.											
47.											
48.											
49.											
50.											
Number of steps scored 3:											

Task Analysis Data Sheet

Program __Rinse car__

Client _____

Instructor _____

Reinforcers _____

Materials _____

Task statement "_____"

Scoring summary

3—without assistance

2—verbal prompt

1—gestural/imitative

0—physical prompt

	Dates								
1. Set wash bucket aside									
2. Get spray gun and turn it on									
3. Move to middle of left side of car									
4. Spray one half of the roof (near side, lengthwise)									
5. Spray near side of car, top to bottom (rear, middle, front)									
6. Spray front windshield, hood, grill, and bumper									
7. Spray far side of car, top to bottom, including roof									
8. Spray rear of car, top to bottom									
9. Take spray gun to car mats									
10. Spray mats									
11. Turn mat over									
12. Spray second side of mat									
13. Turn gun off and return to holder									
14.									
15.									
16.									
17.									
18.									
19.									
20.									
21.									
22.									
23.									
24.									
25.									
Number of steps scored 3:									

Task Analysis Data Sheet

Program __Wipe car_____

Client _____

Instructor _____

Reinforcers _____

Materials _____

Task statement "_____"

Scoring summary

3—without assistance

2—verbal prompt

1—gestural/imitative

0—physical prompt

Dates

1. Get white terrycloth towels	
2. Move to middle of left side of car	
3. Wipe near half of roof	
4. Wipe near side of the car	
5. Wipe the near side of front windshield	
6. Wipe the near side of the hood	
7. Repeat #4–6 on the right side of the car	
8. Wipe the grill and bumper	
9. Wipe the far side of the car, including roof	
10. Wipe the rear of the car	
11. Wipe the rear bumper	
12.	
13.	
14.	
15.	
16.	
17.	
18.	
19.	
20.	
21.	
22.	
23.	
24.	
25.	
Number of steps scored 3:	

Task Analysis Data Sheet

Program __Clean car windows and mirrors__

Client _____

Instructor _____

Reinforcers _____

Materials _____

Task statement "_____"

Scoring summary

3—without assistance

2—verbal prompt

1—gestural/imitative

0—physical prompt

		Dates								
1. Go to cleaning shelf										
2. Get spray window cleaner, newspaper, and paper towels										
3. Use a maximum of three squirts per window										
4. Apply spray to near side of outside windshield										
5. Wipe with newspaper										
6. Polish with paper towel										
7. Apply to far side of outside windshield										
8. Wipe with newspaper										
9. Polish with paper towel										
10. Spray far side of outside of rear window										
11. Wipe with newspaper										
12. Polish with paper towel										
13. Spray near side of rear window on the outside										
14. Wipe with newspaper										
15. Polish with paper towel										
16. Apply spray to outside front side window										
17. Wipe with newspaper										
18. Polish with paper towel										
19. Spray outside rearview mirror										
20. Wipe with newspaper										
21. Polish with paper towel										
22. Open car door										
23. Spray inside side window										
24. Wipe with newspaper										
25. Polish with paper towel										

(continued)

Dates

26. Wipe window molding and vinyl on inside door with paper towel									
27. Wipe chrome on door with paper towel									
28. Spray near side of windshield									
29. Wipe with newspaper									
30. Polish with paper towel									
31. Wipe one half dash, steering wheel, visor and chrome with paper towel									
32. Spray inside rear view mirror									
33. Wipe with newspaper									
34. Polish with paper towel									
35. Get out of car and move to far side front door									
36. Repeat #16–31									
37. Get out of car and move to far side rear door									
38. Spray outside side rear window									
39. Wipe with newspaper									
40. Polish with paper towel									
41. Open door									
42. Spray one half inside rear window									
43. Wipe with newspaper									
44. Polish with paper towel									
45. Wipe window molding, chrome									
46. Spray one half inside rear window									
47. Wipe with newspaper									
48. Polish with paper towel									
49. Clean rear window shelf if not carpet									
50. Move to near side rear door									
51. Repeat steps #38–49									
52. Replace cleaning supplies and pick up towels									
Number of steps scored 3:									

Task Analysis Data Sheet

Program __Vacuum car__
Client _____
Instructor _____
Reinforcers _____
Materials _____
Task statement "_____"

Scoring summary
3—without assistance
2—verbal prompt
1—gestural/imitative
0—physical prompt

		Dates								
1. Take shopvac to car										
2. Plug in vac										
3. Turn on vac										
4. Sit or kneel in right side of front seat, bringing vac to door										
5. Vacuum: seats										
6. carpet										
7. ledges										
8. bottom of doors										
9. ash trays										
10. Vacuum mats if carpet										
11. Repeat steps 4–10 for left side of front seat, left side of rear seat, right side of rear seat										
12. Turn off vac										
13. Pick up floor mats										
14. Place floor mats in appropriate location										
15. Inspect car for dirty spots										
16. Clean off any dirt identified in Step 15										
17. Close doors										
18. Contact supervisor (to move car)										
19.										
20.										
21.										
22.										
23.										
24.										
25.										
Number of steps scored 3:										

Task Analysis Data Sheet

Program __Wax and polish car__

Client _____

Instructor _____

Reinforcers _____

Materials _____

Task statement "_____"

Scoring summary

3—without assistance

2—verbal prompt

1—gestural/imitative

0—physical prompt

	Dates								
1. Locate buffer case and wax									
2. Open case, take buffer out									
3. Turn buffer upside down									
4. Pick up black bonnet (polishing)									
5. Stretch bonnet over polishing pad									
6. Plug buffer into electrical cord									
7. Apply wax to black bonnet									
8. Take wax and buffer to car									
9. Place buffer on car surface, polishing pad down									
10. Turn buffer to "low"									
11. Move buffer in up and down motions on surface to be waxed									
12. Move buffer in side to side motions on surface									
13. When buffer is out of wax, turn off									
14. Take buffer to wax									
15. Apply wax to bonnet									
16. Return buffer to car									
17. Place buffer on car surface									
18. Turn buffer to "low"									
19. Repeat steps #9–18 until entire car surface is waxed									
20. Stop buffer									
21. Unplug buffer									
22. Turn buffer upside down									
23. Remove black bonnet									
24. Rinse black bonnet in water to remove wax									
25. Hang black bonnet on hook to dry									

(continued)

Dates

26. Pick up dry polishing bonnet										
27. Put dry polishing bonnet on buffer										
28. Check car to see that wax is dry										
29. If dry, place buffer right side up on the car surface										
30. Turn buffer to "hi"										
31. Move buffer in up and down motion over car to remove wax (no pressure)										
32. Move buffer in side to side motion over car to remove wax										
33. Remove all wax, turn buffer off and set it down										
34. Get clean dry cloth and dust entire car surface										
35. Turn buffer over and unplug										
36. Remove polishing bonnet and hang up										
37. Pick up buffing bonnet										
38. Place buffer bonnet on head										
39. Plug in buffer										
40. Place buffer on car surface right side up										
41. Turn buffer on "hi"										
42. Move buffer in up and down motion over car surface (no pressure)										
43. Move buffer in back and forth motion over car surface										
44. When the entire car surface has been polished, unplug buffer										
45. Turn buffer upside down										
46. Remove buffing bonnet										
47. Rinse buffing bonnet in water										
48. Hang buffing bonnet up to dry										
49. If there are more cars to wax, repeat steps 9–50										
50. Place buffer in case, put away										
Number of steps scored 3:										

Task Analysis Data Sheet

Program __Clean work area__

Client _____

Instructor _____

Reinforcers _____

Materials _____

Task statement "_____"

Scoring summary

3—without assistance

2—verbal prompt

1—gestural/imitative

0—physical prompt

Dates

1. Pick up and dispose of paper towels and rags in work area										
2. Wring out damp towels and rags										
3. Hose work area (with spray gun)										
4. Check out (time punch)										
5.										
6.										
7.										
8.										
9.										
10.										
11.										
12.										
13.										
14.										
15.										
16.										
17.										
18.										
19.										
20.										
21.										
22.										
23.										
24.										
25.										
Number of steps scored 3:										

Unit IV

SURVIVAL SKILLS

CHAPTER 9

Vocational Survival Skills

OBJECTIVES

To be able to:

1. Define generic and specialized vocational survival skills.
2. List and discuss reasons for developing exit criteria for vocational habilitation programs.
3. Describe how to develop exit criteria.
4. Describe the information needed in order to design a useful training curriculum for a specific job.

This chapter and Chapter 10 cover one of the important differences between the proactive approach and more traditional approaches to vocational rehabilitation. Specifically, the proactive focus is not on changing characteristics that are presumed to be inside the worker such as motivation, but rather on changing the way in which work skills are taught. Thus, in the proactive approach, the focus is on the design of instructional strategies that result in behavior change (Ziarnik, 1980).

CONTENT VERSUS METHOD

Before proceeding, it is important to put this material and the material in Chapter 10 in perspective. These chapters focus on the content of vocational training. As noted in Chapter 3, many methods for achieving successful vocational habilitation are not addressed in this text. This is not to suggest that such methods are unimportant. In fact, a major difference between successful and unsuccessful habilitation programs is usually found by examining how well staff can design and implement behavior change programs. We are so convinced of the importance of sound teaching methods to successful habilitation that the major part of *Behavioral Habilitation Through Proactive Programming* (Bernstein, Ziarnik, Rudrud, & Czajkowski, 1981), was devoted to that very issue. Program designers should consult this and a variety of other sources for current methods of teaching vocational skills (e.g., Bellamy, Horner, & Inman, 1979; Rusch & Mithaug, 1980; Wehman, 1981).

VOCATIONAL SURVIVAL SKILLS

As discussed in Chapter 2, vocational survival skills are: a) directly related to work, and b) necessary in order to maintain successful vocational placement. There are two types of vocational survival skills: generic skills and specialized skills. Generic skills are those which are required on most jobs. For instance, coming to work on time, calling in if you are going to be absent, and appearing to remain on-task, are generic vocational survival skills. Specialized survival skills, on the other hand, are typically required only for a specific job or a specific type of job. For instance, the skills necessary to polish the entire outside of an automobile are required for auto detail work but are unlikely to be needed in most other occupations.

One of the as yet unresolved questions in vocational habilitation is whether it is preferable to teach generic skills prior to teaching specialized vocational skills or whether it is preferable to train both simultaneously. This is obviously an important issue, as it relates to whether or not all vocational habilitation training should be provided on the job. If anything, we are inclined to the opinion that on the job training is more efficient and probably more effective because no generalization across settings is needed.

However, at present, the training of generic vocational survival skills is usually conducted away from actual job settings and prior to specialized vocational skill training. The discussion that follows assumes that your habilitation program is being implemented under such conditions. Our intent is to describe how a proactive approach can be used in existing program structures.

Generic Vocational Survival Skills

Exit Criteria Suppose the goal for trainees who graduate from a vocational habilitation program is to enter on the job training that will teach them specialized vocational survival skills. Both the trainees and their supervisors need a way to determine when an individual is ready to graduate from the generic training program and proceed to specialized training. In other words, program exit criteria are needed that will specify what an individual must do in order to graduate.

As described in Chapter 2, the two primary sources of information on vocational survival skills are: a) the research on variables related to success or failure on the job, and b) generic requirements of jobs in your community. These were the sources used to develop the exit criteria on the Worker Readiness Checklist (Ziarnik, Grupé, Morrison, Conway, Leeming, & Cruchon, 1983) at Goodwill Industries in Denver. The exit criteria are shown in Table 9.1.

Table 9.1. Exit criteria at Goodwill Industries–Denver

Attendance

1. Attends 21 out of 22 possible working days per month
2. Calls in all absences to supervisor within 10 minutes of the beginning of the work day
3. Plans and communicates any work day appointments with supervisor in accordance with company policy
4. Plans and communicates vacation time within acceptable company policy
5. Reaches work place by means of own arrangement (bus, taxi, bike)
6. Punches in and out 100% of time
7. Is at work station on time:
    a. Start of day
    b. Breaks

Work Skills

8. Only brings appropriate work or break materials to work (All nonwork materials are stored in a designated area.)
9. Gets out work materials and begins work immediately
10. Works at assigned task continuously for 1 hour and 50 minutes
11. Is on task 95% of the time observed (*must* look busy)
12. Maintains a consistent 85% productivity rate (waived with physical handicap)
13. Cleans up work area at the end of the day
14. Follows company rules as instructed:
    a. Moves safely through areas
    b. Wears clothing appropriate to workplace
    c. Uses safety devices (e.g., glasses, earplugs, etc.)
15. Keeps body clean and odor free:
    a. Hair
    b. Face
    c. Breath
16. Communicates upon request:
    a. Full name
    b. Address
    c. Home telephone
17. Manages production needs appropriately by either communicating with supervisor or independently getting more materials within 5 seconds of running out of materials

(*continued*)

Table 9.1. *(continued)*

Social Skills

18. Communicates basic needs that may interfere with ability to continue working, such as sickness, pain, or when unable to do job and in need of help
19. When given an instruction:
    a. Makes eye contact
    b. Gives verbal acknowledgment with normal voice tone
    c. Has neutral or pleasant facial expression
    d. Complies within 5 seconds
20. Responds to an instruction that requires compliance for a specified time interval
21. When work performance is corrected by any person identified as authority:
    a. Makes eye contact
    b. Gives verbal acknowledgment with normal voice tone
    c. Has neutral or pleasant facial expression
    d. Corrects mistake within 5 seconds
22. When praised, gives verbal acknowledgment in pleasant tone and returns to work
23. Expresses interpersonal issues or feelings appropriate to workplace in a socially approved manner
24. Gets along (e.g., cooperation, pleasant, etc.) with co-workers without prompts
25. Seeks out and initiates interaction appropriate to workplace with other workers during breaks at least 4 times/week
26. Relates verifiable facts
27. Has only personal or approved items in possession

First, the literature reviewed in Chapter 2 was used to generate a list of likely requirements for job success. Then, employers in the Denver area reviewed the list and indicated which items were important and which were not. Thus, the Goodwill–Denver exit criteria are both community-referenced and scientifically based. They reflect our current knowledge regarding what generic skills are necessary to ensure vocational survival in the Denver area.

Operationalizing Exit Criteria Many of the sample criteria are not completely operationalized. That is, they are not written in observable and measureable terms. This is because a comprehensive operationalized list would be too lengthy to be practical. Consequently, determining whether an individual meets a particular criterion is a two-step process. First, one or more staff rate whether the client meets each of the criteria. Then, staff are required to operationally define each criterion which, in their opinion, has not been met, and take data on the client's performance (see the Sioux Vocational School Social-Interpersonal Behavior Checklist in Chapter 10 for a standardized version of this process). For instance, the criterion, Gets out work materials and begins work immediately, might be operationalized as: Given a work day that begins at 8:15, the individual is on task with all materials for the task at the work station by 8:15 for 20 consecutive working days.

This requirement is extremely important because unreliability of ratings and staff judgments are well known (Bernstein et al., 1981). Do not assume that an individual has not met one of your exit criteria based on staff ratings or judgments. Staff should be required to have behavioral baseline data based on operationalized definitions to justify all programming decisions.

Revising Exit Criteria By the time you read the criteria shown in Table 9.1, it is likely a newer version will be in use at Goodwill–Denver. Development of exit criteria must be an ongoing process for at least two reasons. One is that periodic changes in community-referenced requirements are needed as you become more familiar with job sites in your community and as the number and types of possible jobs for your trainees increase. Direct observation of job sites began after development of the criteria in Table 9.1, so information from those observations will be used in future revisions. The other reason for revising criteria is that new data continue to become available from both published reports and trainee outcomes in your program on variables that influence vocational success.

Production Versus Skill Acquisition If generic skill training takes place prior to on the job training, what type of work will trainees do during that training? Too often, the work produced by trainees becomes a higher priority during training than generic skill acquisition. This usually occurs in programs using paid work at the generic skill training level, primarily subcontract work. The authors suggest not using paid work in order to avoid having production take precedence over training. However, this statement is based upon the assumption that simulated work is only a step prior to the trainee progressing to integrated community-based job sites. Simulated work should never be an end in itself. With this model in mind, it is more important, for example, to teach compliance with supervision than to produce large numbers of widgets. There is no reason why alternatives to paid work cannot look as much like paid work as possible and require as many of the same types of skills as possible. Pasting macaroni on cardboard is appropriate for 5-year-olds, not for adults in vocational training. One way to develop alternatives is to purchase materials that can be used as simulated work, most likely as simulated assembly tasks such as collating, packaging, and circuit board assembly. At Goodwill of Denver, we utilize a number of types of simulated work ranging from pilot light assembly to the assembly of intravenous drip bags. Since vocational habilitation programs are typically nonprofit organizations, they are eligible to purchase materials from state and federal surplus houses. These are an excellent source of simulated work. Also, since you will be using community-based job training sites, materials from those sites can often be used as simulated work.

Another alternative to subcontracts is the cottage industry. If the program can produce a product that requires a wide level of skills depending on the particular task involved, it can be appropriate for many different clients. Thus, it may be possible to engage in work that results in a finished product. However, there are several dangers to the cottage industry approach. One is that if the product to be made is going to bring in large orders, there is a chance that production may take precedence over training. Another problem, of course, is quality control. We recommend only the production of items that are marketable and well made. It is better to ask for charity outright and save the cost of materials than to ask people to pay for inferior products because they are made by the handicapped. This latter practice perpetuates the stereotype that handicapped persons cannot produce well made items. Finally, a cottage industry faces all the problems faced by businesses trying to market a new product. For instance, if your product costs so much to produce that it cannot be sold at a price people will pay, it will never result in profits.

Exercises

9-1. Why does your program need exit criteria?
9-2. What do you need to know before choosing exit criteria for your program? (Assume that your overall goal is to make people employable.)

Answers to Exercises

9-1. You need exit criteria so that you can tell which skills people need training in and when they have successfully completed training.
9-2. You need to know: 1) what research indicates are criteria for successful employment, 2) whether you are training generic vocational skills, specialized ones, or both, and 3) community standards for successful employment.

Specialized Vocational Survival Skills

Specialized vocational survival skills are the skills needed for a particular job. As with generic skills, identification of specialized skills includes determining what the person must do and what the criteria are for satisfactory performance. These criteria are the exit criteria from training to employment. When an individual in on the job training meets all the criteria for the job, it is time to gradually fade out the trainer. When an individual being trained in a simulated setting to do a job in an actual setting meets exit criteria, it is time to gradually fade that person into the actual work setting.

Since the tasks required for a particular job title often vary from employer to employer and across geographic location, community-referencing is a must. Janitors in Lemmon, South Dakota, probably do not have to do exactly the same things as janitors in Baltimore. Also, a janitor in a gas station probably does not have to get things as clean as a janitor in a gourmet restaurant.

FROM SKILLS AND CRITERIA TO CURRICULUM CONTENT

Job Conditions Specification

The discussion of vocational survival skills to this point has addressed the questions of what the successful worker must be able to do. In order to design a useful training curriculum, we must also ask under what conditions vocational survival skills must occur. Consider the differences in working conditions between the following two janitorial positions.

The janitor at Bob's Pump & Service Station works from 9:30 A.M. to 6:00 P.M. The janitor's supervisor is Bob Jones, the owner of the station, who is usually within yelling distance throughout the work day. Bob gives the janitor two or three tasks at a time, checks the work and gives feedback on it when those tasks are completed, and then assigns two or three more. The station is a noisy, cheerful environment. The radio plays a top 40 station continuously and the other employees chat while they work. The level of cleanliness that the janitor is expected to maintain can best be described as "keep the junk and crud from taking over." For instance, trash cans and wastebaskets must be emptied daily, but no one worries about a little dirt clinging to the sides of the cans.

The janitor at Le Gourmet, a very expensive French restaurant, works from midnight to 8 A.M. The supervisor gives the janitor a written list of tasks to be completed during the night and then, having just worked all day, goes home. No one else is in the building during the night. The chef and kitchen help arrive the next morning just as the janitor is going home. Feedback, even delayed feedback, is rarely available to the janitor unless a task is completed unacceptably. The only way the janitor can play music is to bring in a personal radio, as the restaurant's stereo is off limits. As you would expect, the level of cleanliness required is extremely high. The overall standard can be described as "if it's inside Le Gourmet, it's clean enough to eat on."

Clearly, the training you provide for a prospective janitor at Bob's will be different in a variety of ways from the training you provide for a prospective janitor at Le Gourmet. This is true regardless of whether you train only at the job site or train in a simulated setting prior to entering the job site. For example, during on the job training, it will probably take much longer to gradually fade feedback and supervision down to naturally occurring levels at Le Gourmet than at Bob's. If you train in a simulated setting, fading feedback down to naturally occurring levels prior to placement will probably increase the likelihood of success.

Trainee Characteristics and Task Analysis

The importance of task analysis to successful vocational habilitation was discussed in Chapter 3. In recent years, numerous task analyzed curricula have been published that are designed for use by professionals in education and habilitation. The rationale for such packaged curricula is that there is no need for everyone who teaches a skill such as putting on pants to reinvent the task analysis for that skill.

There is, however, one common problem with task analysis that often occurs during curriculum design. It is all too easy to forget that the number of

Table 9.2.   Six-step analysis—wiping tables in restaurant

Steps
1. Take bucket with hot water and rag in it to first table.
2. Lift rag out of water
3. Wring out rag.
4. Wipe entire table.
5. Put rag into bucket.
6. Take bucket to next table.

steps in a task analysis depends on both the task and the individual learning the task. A man who is mildly retarded will probably require fewer steps when learning to sweep than a man who is severely retarded with multiple handicaps. Examples of two different analyses of the same task are shown in Table 9.2 and Table 9.3.

We are not suggesting that commercial task analyses are useless. It is usually less work to adapt a published analysis to meet an individual's needs than to write a new analysis. The important point here is that a published task analysis will not meet every trainee's needs as is. Instead, the curriculum must be adapted to meet the needs of the individual.

Exercises

9-3.   What do you need to know about a job to design a good training curriculum for it?
9-4.   Why is it a bad idea to use the same task analysis for all your clients?

Table 9.3.   Thirteen-step analysis—wiping tables in restaurant

Steps
1. Pick up bucket.
2. Go to first table.
3. Set bucket on left side of table.
4. Pick up rag.
5. Wring out rag.
6. Wipe right side of table.
7. Put rag in bucket.
8. Move bucket to right side of table.
9. Pick up rag.
10. Wring out rag.
11. Wipe left side of table.
12. Put rag in bucket.
13. Go to next table.

Answers to Exercises

9-3. You need to know the required tasks, the quality criteria for those tasks, and common conditions in the work place.

9-4. It's a bad idea because some people will need the task divided into more steps than your original, while others will learn the task in fewer steps.

SUGGESTED ACTIVITIES

1. Review any exit criteria used by your agency. Determine whether the skills listed are generic vocational survival skills, specialized ones, or both. If no criteria exist, develop some.
2. Identify the assessment procedures used in your agency to determine if someone has met exit criteria. Are you satisfied with the fairness and consistency of the assessments? If not, how would you improve them?
3. Specify the job conditions for a job in which you place trainees.
4. The lists of tasks for each of the jobs taught at the Huron Adjustment Training Center are shown in Chapter 8. Pick a job in your community similar to one of those listed and compile a list of required tasks. How does your list compare to the Huron list?

ADDITIONAL RESOURCES

Bellamy, G.T., Inman, D.P., & Horner, R.H. Design of vocational habilitation services for the severely retarded: The specialized training program model. In: L. A. Hamerlynck (ed.), *Behaviorial systems for the developmentally disabled: Institutional, clinic, community environments.* New York: Brunner/Mazel, 1979.

Bellamy, G.T., O'Connor, G., & Karan, O. (eds.). *Vocational rehabilitation of severely handicapped persons.* Baltimore: University Park Press, 1979.

REFERENCES

Bellamy, G. T., Horner, R. H., & Inman, D. P. *Vocational habilitation of severely retarded adults.* Baltimore: University Park Press, 1979.

Bernstein, G. S., Ziarnik, J. P., Rudrud, E. H., & Czajkowski, L. A. *Behavioral habilitation through proactive programming.* Baltimore: Paul H. Brookes Publishing Co., 1981.

Rusch, F. R., & Mithaug, D. E. *Vocational training for mentally retarded adults.* Champaign, IL: Research Press, 1980.

Wehman, P. *Competitive employment: New horizons for severely disabled individuals.* Baltimore: Paul H. Brookes Publishing Co., 1981.

Ziarnik, J. P. Developing proactive direct care staff. *Mental Retardation,* 1980, *18*(6), 289–292.

Ziarnik, J. P., Grupé, R., Morrison, C., Conway, K., Leeming, J., & Cruchon, N. *Worker Readiness Checklist.* Unpublished manuscript, Goodwill Industries, Denver, 1983.

CHAPTER 10

Social
Survival Skills

OBJECTIVES

To be able to:

1. List and explain the ways in which social skill deficits may affect vocational success.
2. Define social skills.
3. Identify the environmental cues involved as well as the type of response required for various social skills.
4. List and explain the key elements of a social skills assessment package.
5. Describe the concepts of overgeneralization and undergeneralization as they apply to social skills.
6. Explain how the concept of community referencing relates to social skill training.

A mildly retarded woman who worked as a chamber maid in a large hotel was required to clean a number of rooms each day. Guests who slept late created a problem since she could not clean their rooms. The technique she employed to deal with this problem involved banging on the guests' doors and using obscene language to roust the guests from their beds. This behavior was reported and she was fired (Greenspan & Shoultz, 1981).

A moderately handicapped trainee stripped old paint and varnish from furniture in the day training center program at a woodshop. Since the stripping operation involved the use of caustic chemicals, he had to wear rubberized gloves to protect his hands. When a visitor would enter the shop, the trainee would stop work, take off his gloves, wash his hands, walk over, and shake hands with the visitor. After greeting the visitor, he would get a new pair of gloves, put them on, and then get back to work. In all, he spent 5–10 minutes away from work for every visitor who came in the shop.

Another handicapped individual was living independently in an apartment. One evening, she was visited by a vacuum cleaner salesman. Before the evening was over, she had agreed to purchase the vacuum cleaner and innumerable deluxe accessories at the bargain price of $850.

In all three anecdotes above, individuals failed to demonstrate adequate and appropriate social skills. This lack of social skill put each person in jeopardy within the community. There are a variety of ways a person can fail to succeed at work and within the community. Some of the most serious kinds of failure are related to deficits in social skills.

Social skills are as important to successful adult community life as vocational skills. Previous chapters have discussed vocational training and assessment as they relate to community-referenced criteria. This chapter discusses the assessment and training of social skills within the same framework.

SOCIAL SKILLS DEFICITS AND VOCATIONAL FAILURE

Deficits in social skills are often related to failure in vocational settings in one or more of the following ways:

1. Inappropriate social skills may interfere with the development of vocational skills.
2. Inappropriate social skills may result in being dismissed from a job.
3. Inappropriate social skills may interfere with independent living.
4. Inappropriate social skills may result in placement in a more restrictive environment. In this situation, vocational skills may become irrelevant since, in these more restrictive environments, there are few opportunities to utilize community-referenced vocational skills.

Interference with Skill Development

Without social skills, the development of other skills may be difficult. For example, someone who cries every time she is corrected either on the job or during training is less employable than a client who responds to criticism by giving verbal acknowledgment in a neutral tone of voice and correcting the mistake immediately. Individuals who display bizzare behaviors when they interact with others are not likely to do well in many training or job situations. For example, individuals who refuse to allow physical guidance by trainers will, of necessity, exclude themselves from a number of training opportunities.

This problem can be further compounded if the trainee responds to the trainer's prompt with a physical attack.

Loss of Job

Loss of job, as we saw in Chapter 2, often may be attributed to social skill deficits. Greenspan and Shoultz (1981) interviewed former employers who had recently fired mentally retarded individuals. Seventeen of the 30 individuals lost their jobs for primarily social reasons. The reasons cited for worker termination included: not listening to the boss, incessant talking, inappropriate conversation, walking in on meetings, fighting and stealing, tardiness, nosey behaviors, lack of motivation, eating off dirty plates, being easily angered, and other inappropriate social behaviors.

Becker, Widener, and Soforenko (1979) identified social/emotional problems as the number one reason for the job failure of developmentally disabled clients. The top three reasons identified by Wehman (1981) for the job failure of handicapped clients were:

1. Exhibiting maladaptive behavior
2. Arguing with the supervisor
3. Poor attendance/tardiness

Finally, Rusch, Martin, Lagomarcino, and Tines (1982) reported that, among clients who could perform job skills at competitive rates, poor social skills were the primary cause of job loss. Skill deficits included inability to interact with co-workers, failure to seek supervisors' help, and physical/verbal abuse to supervisors and co-workers. These studies suggest that many people who lose their jobs do so for lack of appropriate social behavior.

Problems in Independent Living

Another example of the impact of social ability, or the lack of it, is in the area of independent living. Schalock and Harper (1978) found that of handicapped individuals who were successful in independent living, only 9% had problems in social behavior. Ninety percent of the unsuccessful clients, on the other hand, were reported to have behavior problems.

Incidents like the vacuum cleaner purchase described previously are not unusual. Clients who are socially inept are clearly at jeopardy in the community. People in the real world are not likely to be as accepting of maladaptive social behaviors as training staff personnel. For example, an employee who lacks the skills to ask guests to go home early on week nights may come to work unrested and be unable to perform at competitive rates. Furthermore, there are individuals who deliberately take advantage of people displaying naive social behaviors. This can result in situations ranging from the buying of unwanted and unnecessary items to contracting venereal disease or unwanted and unplanned pregnancies.

Social skill deficits certainly are not the only factors that are related to client failure in the community. There is, however, sufficient evidence to conclude that community-based programs need to include social skill training in their curriculum.

Reinstitutionalization

The most severe consequence of inappropriate social skills within a community placement is reinstitutionalization. Pagel and Whitling (1978) studied the characteristics of persons with mental retardation who were readmitted to a state hospital following a community placement. They found that about half of the clients were readmitted to institutional care because they had exhibited maladaptive social behaviors. Furthermore, they found maladaptive behavior to be the most commonly cited reason for reinstitutionalization of individuals over the age of 10. Schalock, Harper, and Genung's (1981) investigation of persons with mental retardation who were returned to the institution also suggests that social-emotional behavior is a significant predictor of reinstitutionalization. Eyman and Call (1977) found that physical violence toward others as well as behaviors that resulted in property damage were social problems that were likely to lead to reinstitutionalization. While problem social behaviors are not the only reason handicapped persons are returned to institutional placements, the occurrence of maladaptive social behavior in the community clearly appears to be a good predictor of institutional readmission (Crawford, Aiello, & Thompson, 1979; Lakin, Hill, Hauber, Bruininks, Heal, 1983).

DEFINING SOCIAL SKILLS

While there is general consensus as to the importance of social interpersonal skills, comparatively little attention has been paid in the research literature to teaching socially appropriate behavior. One of the biggest obstacles to designing programs to improve social-interpersonal skills is that these skills are difficult to define. In fact, there are no universally accepted definitions for the concept "social skills." Social skills have been defined as a hand shake greeting, hygiene skills, smiling, eye contact, dating, interacting with the same and different sex peers, reading, money handling, banking, food preparation, and time-telling (McConkey & Walsh, 1982; Smith & Sykes, 1981). Definitions that include such skills are too broad for the purposes of this chapter.

In our view, social skills are defined in a manner similar to that defined by Jackson, King, and Heller (1981). Specifically:

1. Social skills are limited to skills used when individuals interact with others. Skills such as hand washing, reading, banking, etc., are not included.

2. Social skills are situation specific and they maximize the reinforcement a person receives from others. Behaviors acceptable among family members are not likely to be accepted or reinforced by a grocery clerk (e.g., greeting another with a kiss).

3. A socially skilled person does not exhibit interpersonal behaviors that tend to yield short-term rewards (e.g., stealing an object because you want it) but long-term negative consequences (e.g., jail).

4. Social skills, both verbal and nonverbal, are learned.

Exercises

10-1. List four outcomes of inappropriate social skills. Provide an example of one such outcome.

10-2. Write a definition of social skills.

Answers to Exercises

10-1. 1) Interference with development of other skills, 2) placement in a more restrictive environment, 3) dismissal from a job, and 4) interference with independent living are the four outcomes of inappropriate social skills.

Examples:

1. In the vocational training program, John is learning to assemble a circuit board. At times, John inserts a resistor backwards. When the supervisor tells John to redo the circuit board, John throws his work down and stomps back to his work station and refuses to continue work.

2. Jim hits co-workers. During the past month, there were eight incidents. Jim is no longer enrolled in the vocational training program and was referred to the state hospital for placement.

3. When Sally was "upset" at work, she demanded to see the vice-president. The vice-president came down to the work floor and talked with Sally. On the fourth trip down, the vice-president decided this was not the most cost-efficient use of his time. Sally is now unemployed.

4. Ann, who lives in a group home, is friendly. At the bus stop, she gave her name and phone number to a stranger. The group home has had to develop a working relationship with the local police department and telephone company in efforts to reduce annoyance calls.

10-2. Social skills are those learned, situation-specific interpersonal behaviors that maximize the probability of gaining social reinforcers and minimize the probability of negative consequences.

A number of authors have developed models designed to facilitate research and training in the social skill area (Bates & Harvey, 1978; Bernstein, 1981; Russell & Stiles, 1979). For the purpose of curriculum planning and practical assessment, we suggest a simple two-dimensional model shown in Figure 10.1.

Environmental Cues		
Verbal cues	Place cues	Interpersonal relationship cues

	Verbal cues	Place cues	Interpersonal relationship cues
Expressive language	Answering a trainer's questions	Prayer language in church	Returning the boss's "good morning"
Other communication	Gesturing "I don't know" to a question	Tears at a funeral	Using a "respectful" tone of voice with police
Physical movement	Placing a part appropriately in an assembly task, following the instructions	Going to one's job station and staying there during work periods	Showing affection appropriately for same sex and opposite sex friends

Figure 10.1   Two-dimensional model for social behavior.

The first dimension relates to the type of response required by the individual. The responses required in social situations are varied. They may involve:

1. Expressive language (e.g., answering and asking questions)
2. Other communication (e.g., eye contact, gestures, and tone of voice)
3. Physical movement (e.g., staying busy and following directions)

The second dimension that should be considered by trainers relates to the set of environmental cues under which the client will be expected to respond. There is some evidence that the ability to discriminate between when social responses are appropriate and when they are not in on the job situations may be an important predictor of good vocational adjustment (Greenspan, Shoultz, & Weir, 1981). The ability to recognize environmental cues seems to be critical to social skill development.

It is important, therefore, that curriculum planners identify the environmental factors that should serve as cues for appropriate social behaviors. Trainees need to learn to be sensitive to:

1. Verbal cues (e.g., directions, criticism, praise)
2. Place cues (e.g., church vs. home)
3. Interpersonal relationship cues (e.g., boss vs. co-worker)

Conceptually, social skills may be viewed as two-dimensional. In a simple sense, when the responses required of the trainee and the environmental stimuli that cue those responses are clearly described, we have the information we need to begin developing social skill curricula. In the real world, however, social skills are often more complex. This is because, in any single situation, each dimension may have several facets.

A simple example might involve an employee who is asked to follow directions. The environmental cues that the employee needs to identify in this simple situation may contain more than one element. First of all, the individual may need to recognize that he or she has been given a command. Secondly, one must be sensitive to the relationship between himself or herself and the person giving the instructions. While instructions from one's boss should be followed, instructions from a peer (e.g., Give me all your food.) need not be. The way in which the employee responds to the directions also has several facets. The language, affect, and gestures associated with following directions may be as important (in a social sense) as the physical movement involved. An employee who follows his employer's directions to sweep a floor while mumbling obscenities about the work is not likely to make the boss happy. This kind of a situation would be made worse if the employee made obscene gestures at the boss while sweeping.

Exercise

10-3. Given the two-dimensional model for social behavior shown in Figure 10.1, what are the nine possible types of simple behaviors? Give an example of each type.

Answer to Exercise

10-3. a. Verbal cues—expressive language
           How are you? I'm fine.
       b. Verbal cues—other communication
           Do you want to come along? Shakes head no.
       c. Verbal cues—physical movement
           Put your ashes in the ashtray. Client complies.
       d. Place cues—expressive language
           Yelling at a basketball game.
       e. Place cues—other communication
           Knocking on your supervisor's closed door.
       f. Place cues—physical movement
           Sitting with a friend in the lunch room.
       g. Interpersonal relationship cues—expressive language
           Telling a friend that it is time to get back to work.
       h. Interpersonal relationship cues—other communication
           Looking at the supervisor when she or he is talking.
       i. Interpersonal relationship cues—physical movement
           Shaking hands with strangers.

SOCIAL SKILLS ASSESSMENT

Decisions regarding the degree to which an individual participates in a social skills training program may be based upon a four-part assessment: screening, an instructional pretest, an instructional posttest, and follow-up observations.

Screening

One of the biggest obstacles to designing programs to improve social-interpersonal skills is that there are not practical screening tools available with which to identify individual programming needs in the social-interpersonal skills area (Bernstein, Van Soest, & Hansum, 1982). For example, the Vocational Behavior Checklist (Walls, Zane, & Werner, 1978), which covers 399 skills, is more detailed than necessary for a screening instrument, as is the 133-item Vocational Adaptation Rating Scales (VARS) (Malgady & Barcher, 1980). Further, most items on the VARS checklist fail the dead man test (Chapter 2). By the negative focus on maladaptive behavior, a dead person could appear to score rather well and thus, we are left with the question, What do we want the client to do? The Prevocational Assessment and Curriculum Guide (PACG) (Mithaug, Mar, & Stewart, 1978) is intended for assessing prevocational skills and only has five items that address social skills. Further, this instrument was developed by asking sheltered workshop supervisors what was needed by clients for entry into sheltered work. Thus, it is not referenced to competitive employment. Also, the PACG as well as the MDC Behavior Identification Format (1974) and the San Francisco Vocational Competency Scale (Levine & Elzey, 1968) primarily assess work-related but nonsocial skills. These instruments do not meet our requirements for an adequate social skills checklist. It may, therefore, be necessary for local training programs to develop their own screening instrument. Screening instruments should have the following characteristics.

1. They should be relatively easy to administer.
2. There should be a clear relationship between the items on the screening instrument and the skills needed for survival in local employment settings and in the community in general.
3. There should be a clear relationship between the items on the instrument and the social skill training programs utilized at the training facility. That is, the instrument should provide a general idea of what components of the training program the client may need.
4. They should be flexible enough to identify individual problem areas that are not normally part of the social skills training curriculum.

The Sioux Vocational School Social-Interpersonal Behavior Checklist is an example of a locally developed screening device (Bernstein et al., 1982). This instrument has two components. The first section (Figure 10.2) is a simple checklist designed to identify general deficiency areas. In the second section (Figure 10.3), there is an opportunity to describe identified problem areas in more detail. It is important to note that this second part of the screening device requires direct observation of the client's behavior. That is, the frequency, intensity, or duration of behavior should be observed and reported. This kind of

Client_____Staff name_____Staff position_____

No. hours per week you spent with client_____Where_____

Date_____

	Definite need	Minimally acceptable	Definite strength
1. Maintains good health			
2. Maintains good hygiene			
3. Maintains good appearance			
4. Independently follows structured schedule of activity			
5. Finishes assigned tasks			
6. Independently uses free time constructively			
7. Follows instructions from authority figures			
8. Remains flexible in change of staff or situations			
9. Has realistic expectations of self			
10. Accepts constructive criticism			
11. Tells the truth, is honest			
12. Seeks help when faced with problems			
13. Accepts praise			
14. Seeks attention appropriately			
15. Expresses emotions in a socially acceptable manner			
16. Engages in cooperative tasks or activities when asked			
17. Engages with others in social activities			
18. Relates to members of the opposite sex age-appropriately			

(continued)

Figure 10.2.   Sioux Vocational School Social-Interpersonal Behavior Checklist, section one.

	Definite need	Minimally acceptable	Definite strength
19. Relates to members of the same sex age-appropriately			
20. Exhibits appropriate assertiveness in familiar situations			
21. Exhibits appropriate assertiveness in unfamiliar situations			
22. Obeys community laws			
Additional behaviors			

Figure 10.2. (*continued*)

a screening instrument can provide a basis for evaluating the effectiveness of the program as well as providing direction for further assessment.

Instructional Pretest/Posttest

The second element of the assessment procedure is the instructional pretest. The purpose of the instructional pretest is to establish how well the client can perform on the instructional tasks set forth in the social skill curriculum. The results of the test are used to identify appropriate client placement within the curriculum (Hofmeister, 1976). In short, the results of this test tell trainers where to begin teaching. Figure 10.3 shows the pretest/posttest utilized with the didactic section of the attention-seeking instructional program. A client who has mastered the instructional objectives of that section would perform well on the instrument and would, therefore, not need to be exposed to that element of the teaching program.

The same instrument could be utilized for the third element of the assessment process—the instructional posttest. This element of the assessment is designed to test satisfactory completion of the program objectives.

Follow-Up Observation

The final element of the assessment process is the follow-up observation. The procedures utilized to collect follow-up data would be similar to those described in the screening process. In the setting where the problem behavior had occurred or in the presence of the individuals with whom the problem behavior had occurred, the frequency, intensity, or duration of the behavior would be measured.

There are a number of tests designed to measure social skills that evaluate client performance in comparison to some group standards. While the tests may have value in certain situations, they are generally poor aids in planning a specific instructional program. Knowing that an individual is only slightly below average is really of little value. What trainers need is an assessment

Need described below (from checklist) _____
A. Describe an example of each behavior you have observed that led you to check the
    need listed above.

B. Estimate frequency, intensity, and duration of each behavior described above. Not all
    behaviors will have measurable intensity or duration. Frequencies should be mea-
    sured as number of times a day, week, or month (specify which criterion you are
    using).

C. In what settings do the behaviors occur? (residence, school, community, etc.)

D. With whom does each of the behaviors occur? (peers, work supervisors, residence
    supervisors, strangers, etc.)

E. When do the behaviors occur? (time of day, day of week, etc.)

F. Other comments related to described behaviors

Client _____ Staff _____ Date _____

Figure 10.3. Sioux Vocational School Social-Interpersonal Behavior Checklist, section two.

battery that is clearly related to instruction. First of all, the tests should establish
a person's need to learn the social skills in a curriculum. Secondly, the battery
of tests should determine the relationship between the client's skill level and the
curriculum both before and after training. Finally, information regarding the
effect of the training upon the client's behavior away from the training situation
needs to be gathered. When a test is not based on some fixed curriculum-related
standard, it is probably not well suited to provide informatiion for program
planning.

TEACHING SOCIAL SKILLS

It can be seen that teaching social skills involves learning a complex set of
behaviors as well as responding to a complex set of environmental cues.

To date, researchers have reported some success in teaching many of the
responses associated with social skills. Individuals have been taught appropriate verbal behaviors (Bates, 1980; Gibson, Lawrence, & Nelson, 1976; Matson
& Andrasik, 1982), nonverbal behaviors, and socially appropriate activities
(Turner, Hersen, & Bellack, 1978).

Many social skills training procedures, including some of the programs
cited above (Figure 10.4), contain an instructional phase, followed by mod-

Didactic Instruction → Modeling → Practice → Maintenance

Figure 10.4. Typical social skills training procedures.

eling, role playing, and reinforcement for appropriate behavior. In the didactic phase, the client is instructed in the required response. This phase of instruction employs direct instruction techniques and may be conversational in nature. Information is stated clearly and then direct questions are asked about the information (Close, Irvin, Taylor, & Agosta, 1981). Small units of information are presented sequentially and continued until the client clearly can do or verbally describe the required social behavior when asked to do so. In the modeling phase, a role model performs the behavior to be taught. Sometimes one person is used, though multiple models are often used. When live models are unavailable, film and videotaped models have been employed. During the practice phase of training, the client practices the new response, often under a variety of environmental conditions, and receives feedback on performance. A variety of verbal or graphic techniques have been used to provide this feedback, such as verbally indicating correctness or incorrectness, or presenting the trainee with charted data to indicate progress. The maintenance component can range from a token reinforcement system to self-control procedures designed to maintain the behavior.

An example of this type of program (Figure 10.5) was developed by Sioux Vocational School (Ferrara, Rudrud, & Wick, 1983). The sample program elements shown in the figure are designed to teach clients appropriate ways to seek attention. In the Sioux Vocational School materials, the modeling and practice procedures are combined in one section. The corrections are for use only when a client's first response is incorrect. A skill definition is provided for the trainer at the beginning of each segment.

Overgeneralization/Undergeneralization of Social Skills

There is fairly good evidence that many responses demonstrated by socially skilled individuals may be taught to handicapped clients. Less success has been reported in teaching clients to make fine discriminations among the subtle environmental differences in which social skills must be performed (Jackson, King, & Heller, 1981). Many of the problems associated with this component of social skill training can be attributed to undergeneralization or over-generalization. In a situation where undergeneralization is taking place, the client fails to produce appropriate social responses in situations calling for those responses. In an overgeneralization situation, the client produces social behavior in an inappropriate situation.

Training people to discriminate between situations in which social behaviors are appropriate and those where the same behaviors are inappropriate may be the most difficult and complex area associated with social skill training.

Seeking Attention Training Program

Trainer's Definition of Skill

Seeking attention is the ability to communicate to others that you are present and need to be acknowledged at some level:

1. To solve a situation that poses a threat to you or others (emergencies)
2. To give or get information about a situation that is a nonemergency
3. Wanting to chat or interact socially with others

Teaching Procedure

Emergency Didactic

I = Instructor   C = Client

1. I: An emergency is when someone is hurt, sick, or falls. What is an emergency?
   C: When someone is hurt, sick, or falls.   *Correction*: An emergency is when someone is hurt, sick, or falls. What is an emergency?

2. I: If there is an emergency, you get help from the supervisor right away. Who do you get?
   C: The supervisor.   *Correction*: If there is an emergency, you get help from the supervisor. Who do you get?

3. I: That's right. You get the supervisor right away. When?
   C: Right away.   *Correction*: You get the supervisor right away. When do you get the supervisor?

4. I: You do not wait to get the supervisor? Do you wait?
   C: No.   *Correction:* You do not wait to get the supervisor. Do you wait?

Emergency
Modeling & Practice

I = Instructor   C = Client   N = Staff member assisting instructor

1. I: If (name) cut his or her arm in the shop, you tell the supervisor, "(name) is hurt, come quickly." Like this: (I turns to N) "(name) is hurt, come quickly."
   I: Okay. Your turn. Pretend (name) cut his or her arm. What should you do?
   C: Client turns to N: "(name) is sick, come quickly."   *Correction:* Watch, I'll do it again. (Repeat role play)

2. I: If someone falls down, you tell supervisor, "Someone has fallen down, come quickly." Let's pretend

(*continued*)

Figure 10.5.   Example of a social skills training procedure.

I have fallen. What do you do? (I
should fall to the floor and stay
there.)

C: Client turns to N: "Someone has   *Correction:*   Watch, I'll do it again.
fallen, come quickly."   (Repeat from the beginning)

3. I: If there is an emergency, you get the
supervisor right away—even if the
supervisor is busy, talking on the
phone or to other people, or if the
supervisor is in a meeting.
Let's pretend I just dropped a heavy
book on my foot and I'm hurt. What
do you do?
NOTE: N should be talking on phone
or busy in some other way.

C: Client turns to N, interrupts and   *Correction:* Watch, I'll do it again.
says, "Someone is hurt, come   (Repeat from the beginning)
quickly."

Figure 10.5.   (*continued*)

Research in the area of social skill generalization (Marholin, O'Toole, Touchette, Berger, & Doyle, 1979; Matson & Earnhart, 1981; Neef, Iwata, & Page, 1978) has demonstrated the effects of a variety of training procedures designed to increase the client's ability to identify environmental cues for socially appropriate responses. Much of this work compares the effect of training in the environment where the behavior is to take place with training outside of the natural environment.

While this is a relatively difficult area to program for, it is not impossible. The challenge for trainers is to provide examples of social situations that will allow clients to identify the critical environmental factors that should cue performance of a socially appropriate response.

For example, a moderately handicapped individual had a problem keeping his money. It seems that other clients were continually borrowing his cash. They would approach him and say, "Give me your money." The client would immediately comply. The staff at the facility decided that the client was in need of assertiveness training. Specifically, he needed to learn to say, "No, I need my money." In a few training sessions, the staff taught the client to say, "No, I need my money," to the trainer's request for cash. Later that week, it was reported that the client again did not have his money. The client failed to generalize the training to the real world. The only person to whom the client would refuse a loan was the trainer. At the suggestion of one of the authors, further training was conducted utilizing a variety of persons requesting money in a variety of social situations. After this training, the client no longer gave away his money. Unfortunately, the client now overgeneralized the training. When the collection basket was passed in church, the client said in a loud, clear, and assertive voice, "No, I need my money!" This example demonstrates the complexity of teaching skills that occur under a variety of conditions.

Exercise

10-4. Read the following examples of inappropriate social skills. Label them as either over- or undergeneralizations.
    a.   Sam shakes hands with everyone at every possible opportunity.
    b.   Bill responds to his supervisor's requests but he doesn't pay attention to any other staff members.
    c.   Sally never talks to men at work.
    d.   Don will only work on one work task and refuses to try any others.
    e.   Judy greets every client and staff member (all 180 of them) with a cheerful good morning.
    f.   When Bill talks with his supervisor, he begins every conversation with a hug.
    g.   Whenever a supervisor asks a question or provides positive feedback, Ray says, "I'm sorry."
    h.   When waiting for the bus, Gloria talks to strangers and gives out her phone number so they can call her.

Answer to Exercise

10-4.   a. overgeneralization, b. undergeneralization, c. undergeneralization, d. undergeneralization, e. overgeneralization, f. overgeneralization, g. overgeneralization, h. overgeneralization

Deciding What to Teach

Decisions regarding which target behaviors should be included in a social skills curriculum should be based upon the same criteria as curricular decisions made in other skill areas. That is, training programs should be community-referenced and teach skills that are needed for the client to remain and succeed in the community. Changing maladaptive behaviors that may result in immediate readmission to an institution by teaching alternative responses should be targeted as first priority needs. A client who physically attacks other clients and steals their food may not be around long enough for you to teach anything else to him or her!!

The second priority type of behaviors that trainers need to consider teaching includes those behaviors that facilitate training. A client who cries and lies on the floor kicking his feet each time work is corrected by a trainer is not likely to gain as much from instruction as the client who acts upon constructive criticism.

The third priority area that programmers should consider targeting is behaviors that tend to increase the client's likelihood of vocational success. While many of the behaviors related to staying out of an institution as well as those associated with benefiting from instruction are generic, this element of the program must be locally referenced. It may contain a variety of responses both verbal and nonverbal that are unique to the community and individual job sites. Specific behaviors, required by a local employer, should be included at this level. A client busing tables at a restaurant may be expected by his boss to smile and interact with customers. This sort of a target social behavior is specific to that job in that community. Procedures for identifying these target behaviors were discussed in Chapters 2, 8, and 9.

Figure 10.6 shows the outline of a locally developed social skills curriculum. It should be noted that, in this curriculum, there are more priority 3 content areas than priority 2 or priority 1 areas. That is because the majority of social skill problems documented by this agency occurred in vocational and community settings. These problems might be classified as naive or inept rather than as seriously maladaptive.

Each client's program should be developed with the goals of community survival and vocational success in mind. Choices about which components of a social skills curriculum to teach should be based upon the skills demonstrated by the individual as well as the job for which he or she is training. All trainees need *not* receive training in all skill areas or even in all the skill areas where they have difficulties. Trainers must be careful to place the highest priority upon those behaviors that relate directly to vocational success.

SUGGESTED ACTIVITIES

1. Review placement histories and identify why people were removed to a more restrictive setting (e.g., competitive employment to sheltered work or from sheltered work to an institution). How many lost jobs due to poor social skills?

Priority 1—objectives dealing with behaviors that if not taught will result in removal from the community.

	Sioux Vocational School Checklist item
Obeys community laws	22

Priority 2—objectives that are prerequisites to training

	Checklist item
Seeking attention	14
Compliance	7, 8
Acceptable response to feedback	10, 13
Following a schedule	4, 5

Priority 3—objectives related to vocational and community survival

	Checklist item
Telling the truth	11
Expresses emotions appropriately	15
Learns interactions	16, 17, 18, 19
Use of free time	6
Appropriate assertive behavior	20, 21
Problem-solving	9, 12

Figure 10.6.   Outline of Sioux Vocational School social skills curriculum.

2. Review your existing social skills training program. List the behaviors taught by that program. Classify the behaviors as: a) often needed, b) occasionally needed, and c) rarely needed.
3. Review the Sioux Vocational School Checklist as well as the screening device currently used at your facility. Evaluate all items on both checklists and identify the 10 most useful (job-related) items.
4. Take the Seeking Attention (Figure 10.5) training program and modify it for a problem in your program.

REFERENCES

Bates, P. The effectiveness of interpersonal skills training on the social skill acquisition of moderately and mildly retarded adults. *Journal of Applied Behavior Analysis*, 1980, *13*, 237–248.

Bates, P., & Harvey, J. Social skills training with the mentally retarded. In: O. C. Kaven (ed.), *Habilitation practices with the severely developmentally disabled*, Vol. 2. Madison, WI: Waisman Center, 1978.

Becker, R. L., Widener, Q., & Soforenko, A. Z. Career education for trainable mentally retarded youth. *Education and Training of the Mentally Retarded*, 1979, *14*, 101–105.

Bernstein, G. S. Research issues in training interpersonal skills for the mentally retarded. *Education and Training of the Mentally Retarded*, 1981, *16*, 70–73.

Bernstein, G. S., Van Soest, E., & Hansum, D. A social interpersonal behavior screening instrument for rehabilitation facilities. *Vocational Evaluation and Work Adjustment Bulletin*, 1982, *15*, 107–111.

Close, D., Irvin, L., Taylor, V., & Agosta, J. Community living skills instruction for mildly retarded persons. *Exceptional Education Quarterly*, 1981, *2*, 75–85.

Crawford, J., Aiello, J., & Thompson, D. Deinstitutionalization and community placement: Clinical and environmental factors. *Mental Retardation*, 1979, *17*, 59–63.

Eyman, R. K., & Call, T. Maladaptive behavior and community placement of mentally retarded persons. *American Journal of Mental Deficiency*, 1977, *82*, 137–144.

Ferrara, J., Rudrud, E., & Wick, J. *Sioux vocational social skills training program.* Sioux Falls, SD: Sioux Vocational School, 1983.

Gibson, F. W., Lawrence, P. S., & Nelson, R. O. Comparison of three training procedures for teaching social responses to developmentally disabled adults. *American Journal of Mental Deficiency*, 1976, *81*, 379–387.

Greenspan, S., & Shoultz, B. Why mentally retarded adults lose their jobs: Social competence as a factor in work adjustment. *Applied Research in Mental Retardation*, 1981, *2*, 23–38.

Greenspan, S., Shoultz, B., & Weir, M. M. Social judgment and vocational adjustment of mentally retarded adults. *Applied Research in Mental Retardation*, 1981, *2*, 335–346.

Hofmeister, A. *Educating the mildly handicapped.* Logan: Utah State University, 1976.

Jackson, H. J., King, N. J., & Heller, V. R. Social skills assessment and training for mentally retarded persons: A review of research. *Australian and New Zealand Journal of Developmental Disabilities*, 1981, *7*, 113–123.

Lakin, K. C., Hill, B. K., Hauber, F. A., Bruininks, R. H., & Heal, L. W. New admissions and readmissions to a national sample of public residential facilities. *American Journal of Mental Deficiency*, 1983, *88*, 13–20.

Levine, S., & Elzey, F. F. *San Francisco Vocational Competency Scale.* New York: The Psychological Corporation, 1968.

McConkey, R., & Walsh, J. An index of social competence for use in determining the service needs of mentally handicapped adults. *Journal of Mental Deficiency Research*, 1982, *26*, 47–61.

Malgady, R. G., & Barcher, P. R. *Vocational Adaptation Rating Scales (VARS) Manual.* Los Angeles: Western Psychological Services, 1980.

Marholin, D., O'Toole, K. M., Touchette, P. E., Berger, P. L., & Doyle, D. A. I'll have a Big Mac, large fries, coke, and apple pie, . . . or teaching adaptive community living skills. *Behavior Therapy*, 1979, *10*, 236–245.

Materials Development Center. *MDC Behavior Identification Format.* Menomonie: Materials Development Center, Department of Rehabilitation and Manpower Services, University of Wisconsin–Stout, 1974.

Matson, J., & Andrasik, F. Training leisure-time social interaction skills to mentally retarded adults. *American Journal of Mental Deficiency*, 1982, *86*, 533–542.

Matson, J. L., & Earnhart, T. Programming treatment effects to the natural environment. *Behavior Modification*, 1981, *5*, 27–38.

Mithaug, D. E., Mar, D. K., & Stewart, J. E. *The prevocational assessment and curriculum guide.* Seattle: Exceptional Education, 1978.

Neef, N., Iwata, B. A., & Page, T. J. Public Transportation training: In vivo versus classroom instruction. *Journal of Applied Behavior Analysis*, 1978, *11*, 331–344.

Pagel, S. E., & Whitling, C. A. Readmissions to a state hospital for mentally retarded persons: Reasons for community placement failure. *Mental Retardation*, 1978, *16*, 164–166.

Rusch, F. R., Martin, J. E., Lagomarcino, T., & Tines, J. *Why entry level workers lose their jobs: A comparison between mentally retarded and non-handicapped employees.* Paper presented at the Association for Behavior Analysis convention, Milwaukee, May, 1982.

Russell, R. L., & Stiles, W. B. Categories for classifying language in psychotherapy. *Psychological Bulletin*, 1979, *86*, 404–419.

Schalock, R. L., & Harper, R. S. Placement from community-based mental retardation programs: How well do clients do? *American Journal of Mental Deficiency*, 1978, *83*, 240–247.

Schalock, R. L., Harper, R. S., & Genung, T. Community integration of mentally retarded adults: Community placement and program success. *American Journal of Mental Deficiency*, 1981, *85*, 478–488.

Smith, H. M., & Sykes, S. C. Parents' view on the development of social competencies in their mildly intellectually handicapped adolescents. *Australian and New Zealand Journal of Developmental Disabilities*, 1981, *7*, 17–25.

Turner, S. M., Hersen, M., & Bellack, A. S. Social skills training to teach prosocial behavior in an organically impaired and retarded patient. *Journal of Behavior Therapy and Experimental Psychiatry*, 1978, *9*, 253–258.

Walls, R. T., Zane, T., & Werner, T. J. *The Vocational Behavior Checklist.* Morgantown: West Virginia Rehabilitation Center, 1978.

Wehman, P. *Competitive employment: New horizons for severely disabled individuals.* Baltimore: Paul H. Brookes Publishing Co., 1981.

Index